WHAT

COLLECTED POEMS

1980-2009

ESSENTIAL POETS SERIES 166

MARIA MAZZIOTTI GILLAN

WHAT WE PASS ON

COLLECTED POEMS

1980-2009

GUERNICA

TORONTO – BUFFALO – CHICAGO – LANCASTER (U.K.)

2010

Antonio D'Alfonso, editor
Guernica Editions Inc.
P.O. Box 117, Station P, Toronto (ON), Canada M5S 2S6
2250 Military Road, Tonawanda, N.Y. 14150-6000 U.S.A.

Distributors:
University of Toronto Press Distribution
5201 Dufferin Street, Toronto (ON), Canada M3H 5T8
Gazelle Book Services, White Cross Mills, High Town, Lancaster LA1 4XS U.K.

Printed in Canada

Legal Deposit – Second Quarter
Library of Congress Catalog Card Number: 2010923273
Library and Archives Canada Cataloguing in Publication
Gillan, Maria M.
What we pass on : collected poems, 1980-2009 /
Maria Mazziotti Gillan.
(Essential poets series ; 166)
ISBN 978-1-55071-304-6
I. Title. II. Series: Essential poets series ; 166
PS3557.I375W43 2010   811'.54   C2010-901909-1

Contents

WHERE I COME FROM

1995

Betrayals 15

Letter to My Son 17

The Paper Dolls 18

Public School No. 18 Paterson, New Jersey 20

My Daughter at Fourteen: Christmas Dance 22

Awakening 23

The Shadow Rushing to Meet Us 24

Jennifer 26

Letter to My Mother: Past Due 27

To Zio Guillermo: in Memoriam 29

Image in a Curved Glass 30

Eulogy to Blasberg's Farm 32

Waiting for the Results of a Pregnancy Test 33

In New Jersey Once 35

Poem to John: Freshman Year, Drew University, 1983 36

Dawn 38

The Onion 39

Stereopticon 40

Morning in New Jersey 41

Oak Place Musings 42

After the Children Leave Home 44

Love Poem to My Husband 45

The Morse Code of Love 47

Uncertainties 49

Talismans 50

This Shell 51

Christmas Shopping for My Mother, December, 1985 52

God Is Not Easy 54

Mrs. Sinnegan's Dogwood 56

Arturo 58

The Young Men in Black Leather Jackets 60

Growing Up Italian 62

In Memory We Are Walking 65

In the Still Photograph, Paterson, New Jersey, Circa 1950 67
Connections 69
My Grandmother's Hands 71
The Crow 73
17th Street: Paterson, New Jersey 75
Paterson: Alpha and Omega 76
Eighth Grade 79
My Sister 81
Thinking About the Intricate Pathways of the Brain 82
Columbus and the Road to Glory 84
The Leavetaking 88
Out of the Window of My Classroom 90
Lament for Lost Time 91
Home Movies 92
Generations 94
Song for Caroline 95
Paradise Motel 98
Requiem for a Four-Year-Old 100
In Falling Light, Paterson 102
Ma, Who Told Me You Forgot How To Cry 103
But I Always Got Away 105
Ma, I Think of You Waiting 106
Visiting My Mother 108
Grief 110
Heritage 112
On Reading Susan Toth's *Blooming* 113
Where I Come From 114

THINGS MY MOTHER TOLD ME
1999

Learning Grace 117
I Dream of My Grandmother and Great Grandmother 118
My Son Tells Me Not to Wear My Poet's Clothes 120
My Lucky Dress 121
Signs 122
Brushing My Mother's Hair 124

Singing to My Mother 125
My Mother's Garden 127
Mothers and Daughters 130
My Son, that Gray-Eyed Dreamer 131
Passing It On 132
Papa, Where Were You? 134
This Is No Way to Live 136
No One Speaks His Language Anymore 137
My Father Always Smelled of Old Spice 138
This Morning 140
In the Extravagant Kingdom of Words 141
Opening the Door: 19th Street, Paterson 142
Learning Silence 143
The Surprise Party 145
Training Bra 147
Zia Concetta and Her Whalebone Corset 148
First Dance at the CYO 150
First Trip to the Jersey Shore: Long Branch, New Jersey 151
Glittering As We Fall 153
You Were Always Escaping 155
Marilyn Monroe and My Sister 157
My Father's First Car 158
The Moment I Knew My Life Had Changed 160
When We Were Girls 162
My Funny Valentine 164
Work 165
My First Car 167
The Family Car 168
Family Vacations 171
Secrets 174
The Perfect Mother 176
The Two-Dollar Housedress 178
In the Pages of a Photo Album 180
If I Had The Courage, I'd Ask My Children What They Remember
    About Me When They Were Growing Up 182
Yesterday 184
Love Poem to My Husband of Thirty-One Years 186
The Ghosts in Our Bed 188
Love Poem to My Husband 189

Poem to My Husband of Thirty-Three Years 190
In My Home There Are No Angels 191
In La Casa de las Americas 194
The Black Bear on My Neighbor's Lawn in New Jersey 196
The River at Dusk 197
Laura 198
Because Poem for Caroline 200
To My Granddaughter Caroline 202
To My Grandson Jackson on His Second Birthday 203
To Jackson on Your Third Birthday 204
My Mother Gave Me Her Ring 206
Piecework 208
Daddy, We Called You 211

ITALIAN WOMEN IN BLACK DRESSES

2004

Black Dresses 217
Blessed 219
Perspectives 220
The Past 222
After School on Ordinary Days 224
Sunday Mornings 225
My First Room 227
Gym Class 229
Kitchen 233
Taking a Risk 234
Halloween Costume 236
I Want to Write a Love Poem 238
Parties 239
Magic Circle 241
My First Date 242
Cafeteria 244
In the Stacks of the Paterson Public Library 246
The Bed I Remember 248
What I Didn't Learn in School 250
Dorothy 252
Bed 253

Going to the Movies 254
Learning to Sing 256
My Mother Who Could Ward Off Evil 258
My Father Always Bought Used Cars 259
Cheap 260
So Many Secrets 262
Winter Dusk 264
When I Was a Young Woman 266
The Cup 266
My Mother-in-Law 269
Nail Clippings 271
Poem to John 274
Window 277
Rainbow Over the Blue Ridge Mountains 278
Return 279
Song in Praise of Spring 280
Elvis Presley Is Alive and Well on Lincoln Avenue in Fair Lawn, New
    Jersey 281
The Herald News Calls Paterson a Gritty City 282
The Great Escape 284
Noise 286
What I Do Is 287
Breathing 289
Sometimes I Forget That You Are Dead 291
This Leaf 293
I Don't Know 295
The Story of My Day 297
In My Family 299
Doris Day 301
Nancy Drew, I Love You 303
Last Night My Mother Came Back 306
Laura, Now That You Are Gone 308
Since Laura Died 310
The Studebaker Silver Hawk 312
Signposts 314
A Geography of Scars 316
In the New Millennium 317
When I Leave You 319
Grief 321

These Are the Words I Have Said 323
Traveler's Advisory 325
Water Chestnut 326
How to Turn a Phone Call into a Disaster 328
This Morning 331
Shame 333
Donna Laura 335
Learning How to Love Myself 337

ALL THAT LIES BETWEEN US
2007

People Who Live Only in Photographs 341
Little House on the Prairie 343
What Did I Know About Love 345
The Mediterranean 346
Christmas Story 347
There Was No Pleasing My Mother 349
Breakfast at IHOP 351
I Want to Write a Poem to Celebrate 352
Superman 353
I Am Thinking of the Dress 355
My Father's Fig Tree Grew in Hawthorne, New Jersey 357
My Sister and Frank Sinatra 359
Sunday Dinners at My Mother's House 361
My Father Always Drove 363
Spike-Heels 365
Trying to Get You to Love Me 366
Housework and Buicks with Fins 369
Driving into Our New Lives 371
Nighties 372
In the Movies No One Ever Ages 374
Who Knew How Lonely the Truth Can Be 375
I Wish I Knew How to Tell You 377
What a Liar I Am 379
On an Outing to Cold Spring 381
Selective Memory 383
Your Voice on the Phone Wobbles 385

On Thanksgiving This Year 388
I Never Tell People 390
Do You Know What It Is I Feel? 393
What I Remember 395
I Walk Through the Rooms of Memory 397
Nothing Can Bring Back the Dead 399
What I Can't Face About Someone I Love 401
Is This the Way It Is with Mothers and Sons? 403
Everything We Don't Want Them to Know 405
At Eleven, My Granddaughter 406
My Daughter's Hands 408
My Grandson and GI Joe 410
What We Pass On 412
The Dead Are Not Silent 414
What the Dead No Longer Need 416
I Want to Celebrate 417
Couch Buddha 418

NEW POEMS
2008

In My Remembered Childhood 421
Shame Is the Dress I Wear 423
City of Memory, Paterson 425
It's Complicated, This Loving Now, 427
What Do My Hands Reach For? 429
The Polar Bears Are Drowning 426
My Grandchildren in Dallas 430
Playing with Dolls 433
The Moments That Shine 434
How Many Ghosts Can Gather in One House? 435
What the Body Knows 436
Imagine 1979 437

WHERE I COME FROM

1995

Betrayals

At thirteen, I screamed,
"You're disgusting,"
drinking your coffee from a saucer.
Your startled eyes darkened with shame.

You, one dead leg dragging,
counting your night-shift hours,
you, smiling past yellowed, gaping teeth,
you, mixing the eggnog for me yourself
in a fat dime store cup,

how I betrayed you,
over and over, ashamed of your broken tongue,
how I laughed, savage and innocent,
at your mutilations.

Today, my son shouts,
"Don't tell anyone you're my mother,"
hunching down in the car
so the other boys won't see us together.

Daddy, are you laughing?
Oh, how things turn full circle,
my own words coming back
to slap my face.

I was sixteen when you called one night from your work.
I called you "dear,"
loving you in that moment
past all the barriers of the heart.
You called again every night for a week.

I never said it again.
I wish I could say it now.

Dear, my Dear,
with your twisted tongue,
I did not understand you
dragging your burden of love.

1980

Letter to My Son

The weeks tumble over themselves
since you've been gone. The leaves
fall from the oaks.
The air turns damp and biting,
the sky gray as an old blanket.

We are unchanged, moving
in our accustomed circles.
You, miles away, have grown into a man
I can be proud of; but when you call,
I feel I am speaking to a person
hidden behind a screen. I remember

you as a little boy, your legs chunky,
your eyes gray and dreamy as a Turner
landscape. A figure moves toward you,
a younger version of myself.
She holds your hand. You speak.

Other scenes appear. She stands
at the bottom of the stairs,
calls "In a minute, in a minute,"
till your eyes close in sleep.

The weeks go by.
You spin your life into shape.
Now it is you who chant,
"In a minute, in a minute,"
and I who taste salt on my tongue.

The Paper Dolls

To my sister Laura

Dark-eyed Julio laughed his way
into our house, swung me in air.
He said: "This one is my girl"
and "I'll wait for you. Will you marry me?"

I held my mother's hand
when he married.
I never looked at his bride
or said their names.
On the way out of the church,
past confetti and congratulations,
I threw up on Mrs. Gianelli's fur coat.
She never forgave me.

We ate fresh snow with espresso on it,
sugar sprinkled on top. Nothing since
has tasted so good.

Your breasts grew first.
You were older, destined for 36D.
I wondered why you weren't ashamed.
My own grew round as oranges, then stopped.
I was glad.

No matter what you did, men grabbed
at you, cornered you in hallways
and kitchens, thought your breasts
were a sign, wanted to drink,
to unsnap your bra.
I followed you everywhere.

We rode in Carmela's old Ford
through Bergen County dreaming.
Dreaming the lovely houses were ours,
dreaming a prince would save us.

Now in your September kitchen, I watch you
twist your hands. We are close
though we rarely speak. Those rides
in summer and winter, hopes that beat
like caged birds in our hearts,
remain stored in boxes, the lids
never open. Your body is twisted by disease;
mine bends forward as though I wait for blows.

Once I envied your breasts
as you envied my poems.
Life has flattened us both out,
turned us into cardboard figures
like our paper dolls
stiff and easily torn.

Public School No. 18
Paterson, New Jersey

Miss Wilson's eyes, opaque
as blue glass, fix on me:
"We must speak English.
We're in America now."
I want to say, "I am American,"
but the evidence is stacked against me.

My mother scrubs my scalp raw, wraps
my shining hair in white rags
to make it curl. Miss Wilson
drags me to the window, checks my hair
for lice. My face wants to hide.

At home, my words smooth in my mouth,
I chatter and am proud. In school,
I am silent, grope for the right English
words, fear the Italian word
will sprout from my mouth like a rose,

fear the progression of teachers
in their sprigged dresses,
their Anglo-Saxon faces.

Without words, they tell me
to be ashamed.
I am.
I deny that booted country
even from myself,
want to be still

and untouchable
as these women
who teach me to hate myself.

Years later, in a white
Kansas City house,
the Psychology professor tells me
I remind him of the Mafia leader
on the cover of *Time* magazine.

My anger spits
venomous from my mouth:

I am proud of my mother,
dressed all in black,
proud of my father
with his broken tongue,
proud of the laughter
and noise of our house.

Remember me, Ladies,
the silent one?
I have found my voice
and my rage will blow
your house down.

1984

My Daughter at Fourteen:
Christmas Dance

Panic in your face, you write questions
to ask him. When he arrives,
you are serene, your fear
unbetrayed. How unlike me you are.

After the dance,
I see your happiness; he holds
your hand. Though you barely speak,
your body pulses messages I can read

all too well. He kisses you goodnight,
his body moving toward yours, and yours
responding. I am frightened, guard my
tongue for fear my mother will pop out

of my mouth. "He is not shy," I say. You giggle,
a little girl again, but you tell me he
kissed you on the dance floor. "Once?"
I ask. "No, a lot."

We ride through rain-shining 1 A.M.
streets. I bite back words which long
to be said, knowing I must not shatter your
moment, fragile as a spun-glass bird,

you, the moment, poised on the edge of
flight, and I, on the ground, afraid.

Awakening

I wake slowly, closed against the eyes
of morning. Your pillow is still warm.
The children sleep, flushed and damp,
in their beds.

The clock ticks smoothly.
The milk glasses wait in the sink.

My mother got up early
in the frozen mornings.

My day's dawning was her
eyes and hands loving me awake.

In memory, the farina still steams.
The stove murmurs. The bread
rises sweetly in its bowl.
I am safe in a circle of love.

The oak creaks and is silent.
My rooms are still.

Listen for my heartbeat.
Am I breathing?

1980-84

The Shadow Rushing to Meet Us

For Jennifer

My just turned fourteen was novels
through which I dreamed my hours away,
and an innocence ferocious in its blindness.
My fourteen was Sinatra records and Billy
Eckstein's syrupy voice and long gray skirts
that stopped just short of rolled bobby socks.
My fourteen was shiny little girl hair,
no style springing curly hair.

Your fourteen is Vanderbilt jeans
and Sassoon shirts, your blonde hair
perfectly ironed into curls, your cornflower
eyes, the lids blue-shadowed, bright
as sun-beaten glass. Your woman
body sends animal signals I have not learned, even now.

Yet when I drive through the dark Allendale streets
to pick you up from the dance, in the carlight,
your face, eyes are taut, shuttered. We drop Colleen
at her house. You cry. The opaque veil in
your eyes melts.

I remember a dance, a high school dance...
I stood all night on the sidelines alone. The smile
scaled from my face like old glue. My new red blouse
and plaid skirt could not cover my nakedness
as I, standing stupidly, no longer even trying
to smile, brushed away tears
as you do now. Watching your face, pleated
with anguish, I see that my fourteen and yours

are not so far apart after all. We sit in our
kitchen. I hold you, smooth away your tears,

try to tell you how we all come to it
in the end, the brick wall, the shadow
rushing to meet us.

So it is not so bad to cry now here in my arms, safe...
a dress rehearsal for the real tears
which will come sure as rain.

Jennifer

Under the luscent skin,
the fine bones, your mind,
fierce and sharp, bites
into questions while
your quick heart cries
for all lame things,
yet you fear your beauty
is only an accident
of genes colliding.

"But when they know me,"
you say, "when they know me,
they won't like me."

Daughter, hear me.
I proclaim your loveliness,
clutching your poems
in your hand, breathing
fire, I draw closer, warm
my cold hands, want
to remember you like this,
so alive I could strike
a match off your face.

Letter to My Mother: Past Due

Today you tell me your mother appears
to you in dreams, but she is always
angry. "You're wrong," she screams.
You see her as a sign;
when she visits your nights, a cloud
of catastrophe bursts on your house.

Ma, hearing you tell me about her,
I see you, for a moment, as a young
girl, caught in a mahogany frame,
a young girl in a thirties wedding
dress with a crown of flowers in your
hair, your eyes deep and terrified,

see you leaning on the rail of that phantom
ship, waving one last goodbye, think
of you, writing to her, year after year,
sending her stilted photographs of your
children, a photo of yourself, your body
young and firm in a flowered dress.

You never saw her again.
She comes to you now only in dreams, angry she
comes. Did she, once, show her love as you
do, scolding, always scolding, yet always
there for me as no one else has ever been?

Once, twenty years ago, a young man bought
my dinner (oysters and wine and waiters
with white cloths draped over their arms),
forced his way into my room in that seedy
Baltimore hotel, insisted he would teach me
how to love, and as I struggled, you called,

asked, "What's wrong? I know something's
wrong." I didn't understand how you could have known.

Yet even now, you train your heart on us like radar,
sensing our pain before we know it ourselves
as I train my heart on my children.

Promise me, Ma, promise to come to me in dreams,
even scolding, to come to me though I have been angry
with you too often, though I have asked you
to leave me alone. Come to me in dreams,
knowing I loved you
always, even when I hurled my rage in your face.

To Zio Guillermo: In Memoriam

I forget him for years,
his shadow kindling on sunset,
his voice gravelly, his hands,
nicotine-stained and calloused,
shaping a silver ball for me

out of cigarette papers, first
small, then layer on layer, our
days silvered, the Camels consumed,
one after the other, his hands
never free of the curling smoke,

his warm smoke smell. In the summer
evenings, his hands carve intricate
bird houses, scrolled and latticed,
and wind pointers, black birds with
whirling wings. Curls of pine

beard his feet. His eyes say
I am all he has of child, this godfather
uncle, his harridan wife shoving him
through days, his eyes mild and sad.

Though he is dead now ten years,
I see him still, rustling through
corn in our bright patchwork garden,
bending over zinnias and marigolds,
calling the birds home.

1981

Image in a Curved Glass

Janet of the freckles and the pale white skin,
Janet of the board body and knobby knees,
I remember your eyes, round and dark as raisins,
your father, runty and plain, just like you.

In your little room, we whispered behind closed doors,
laughed into mirrors, clutched our hoped-for beauty
and ventured out into the sun. We never talked
about your grandmother dying in the room next to yours,
her eyes blazing, the stench permeating the hall,

or your step-mother who blossomed
miraculously with child. What did you think
of as you lay in that iron bed in your lopsided little
house with its thin walls? You never said.

In your lace graduation dress stretched
tight across bud breasts, your face was plain
as a plank wearing lank brown hair.
That summer you moved to Pompton Lakes,
I took the bus to visit you once
and you showed me your new house, small
and narrow as the 13th Street one, but with a brook
out back where we ate watermelon
dripping seeds into sweet grass. We walked the town's
crooked streets while you whispered that you had
a boyfriend named Ron and you loved him.
Two years later, when my life had
filled out with friends and school, you came to visit.
We went together to the Blue Stamp Redemption
Center where you turned in your hoarded books
for an iron and talked of plans to marry Ron
and of waiting for his letters though sometimes

they did not come. Your life seemed to me
then strange as a Martian's yet even in my separateness,
I saw your loneliness like a rift in the sky,
saw a vision of your Pompton house

where your stepmother gave birth interminably
to babies who squeezed you out until you drifted away.
Even then, I knew you had done it already
but I did not ask. We never talked about the things
that mattered. The cells of thirty years have been
brushed from my hands

yet I wonder still: Did he marry you? Did you pop
one child after another in rented rooms?

Eulogy to Blasberg's Farm

We used to reach it, take our
bikes up Lynack Road, pause
at gravestones in the bramble-
bushed cemetery, stones old
and fallen, wild flowers growing
over them in tangled clumps.

We sat cross-legged on the grass,
drinking our Cokes, preparing
for a journey whose distances
we could not even begin to measure.

Up Lynack Road into the back gate
of Blasberg's, we rode the crooked
rows, drowning in scented
apples, deep and scarlet
against a lilac-colored sky.

We careened down
the road, spring flying behind
us like a cloak, unaware that one
day we would mourn the tangled
underbrush, the lost curve
of apple trees, the blue
untarnished sky.

1983

Waiting for the Results of a Pregnancy Test

At forty-one, I am uncertain of more things
than I could have imagined twenty years ago.

Your existence or non-existence
hovers over me today. The voices
of the world, my friends the liberated
women who are close to me, cry
abort abort abort in unison.

Yet the voice inside me shouts
            No

shows my selfishness in its mirror
my soul's dark intent.

This newt, this merging of tiny cells
makes an explosion like comets
colliding in my ordered universe.

I want to say: I'm too old, too tired,
too caught up in trying wings so long unused,
but that voice will not be silent. It beats
in my bones with its primitive insistence.

Little life, floating in your boat of cells,
I will carry you under my heart
though the arithmetic is against us both.

Today I bypass the baby departments,
the thousand reminders that come to me now.
The young women wheeling strollers through
Bradlees, the girl in the maternity shirt
which proclaims: "I'm not lonely anymore."

I want to scream, we are all born lonely,
and the child beating under our hearts
does not change that. I want to lie down
on the ugly pebbled floor of Bradlees and kick
my feet and pound my fists and make this intruder
in my life vanish.

As I stand at the checkout line, I see our years unroll:

the bottles
midnight feedings
tinker toys
baseball games
PTA meetings

are boulders in my path, a mountain
of boulders I will have to climb
for you. I walk into the spring sunlight
while my life snaps closed around me and my fear.

My friends are all my age, their children in high school
as mine are. I will be alone with you.
You will be born with a scowl on your face,
your hands shaking, having taken from the marrow
of my bones my own quaking.

We will rock together in this leaky boat and
I will love you, I know; it is only in these first
moments, while I alter the picture of my life
I had painted with such sure strokes, only in these
moments that I wish you were not there.

In New Jersey Once

In New Jersey once, marigolds grew wild.
Fields swayed with daisies.
Oaks stood tall on mountains.
Powdered butterflies graced the velvet air.

Listen. It was like that.
Before the bulldozers.
Before the cranes.
Before the cement sealed the earth.

Even the stars, which used to hang
in thick clusters in the black sky,
even the stars are dim.

Burrow under the blacktop,
under the cement, the old dark earth
is still there. Dig your hands into it,
feel it, deep, alive on your fingers.

Know that the earth breathes and pulses still.
Listen. It mourns. In New Jersey once, flowers grew.

Poem to John: Freshman Year, Drew University, 1983

You've been gone now four weeks.
It seems like forever.
You say you'll call.
I wait near the phone
so I won't miss you.
The phone stays mute.

I feel the way I did
when I let you walk home
from kindergarten
and you were late.

Only now you're grown-up
and you're doing fine.
I'm the one who can't let go,
who can't stop trying to help you,
who can't stop

trying
because you're grown-up
and I have to not
remind you to get your shot,
and I have to not bring you blankets
and peanut butter and potato chips
and chocolate chip cookies

and I have to keep my voice down
when I see you making the same mistakes
I made.
I sit near the phone, waiting,
needing to hear from you
but not wanting to shame you by calling.

The truth is you're more grown-up than I am, and I'll try to believe what I know already. You'll be fine without me. You'll be fine.

Dawn

Here, in the early morning,
with rain running from the
gutters, the loneliness

fits like a comfortable coat
and the quiet, familiar creakings
of the house are part of me.

I am soothed by them, the sounds and
stirrings, water in the bath,
my son's footsteps on the stairs.

The sleeves of this coat are warm
on my skin. My house of bones rests
calm and singing a music all its own.

The Onion

To Robert Bly

Shaded in layers from burnt umber to pumpkin to gold, this onion curves upward in a graceful arc, the line of a womb perhaps or the shape people draw to represent women. Curved and rounded in on itself, only one burnt orange strip of skin, frail as parchment, flaps loose, pointing down and away. The rest, layer on layer, protects its heart. I am like that, private as a bud, wound tight, circling in on itself.

We are all like that, yet peel us away, one layer at a time, and underneath, at the core, each of us with a secret to tell, burning under the bleached scalp. I hold this earth fruit in my hand. Pumpkin-colored lines flow upward toward the tip, never wavering in

their journey as though flowing from some hidden river. Why are we so much more than we appear to be? Touch the veined skin, the cool roundness. We cannot know its secrets. It does not murmur as a shell murmurs; it keeps to itself, wrapped in its thin skin, frail and ferocious as a sparrow. Even the stars dim watching us, our backs to the wall.

1981

Stereopticon

All the people from my past come to sit with me tonight in my bright suburban kitchen, Ma, in her rocker, holding me still, telling her stories, and Daddy like dark wine, and Laura, her laugh clear as a crystal bell, and Al, his small brown hand in mine, and Zia Louisa with her huge chocolate squares, and Zia Rosa, the nights under the grape arbor, its summer sweet smell, and Zia Amalia, the mole on her nose, her foot tapping its nervous rhythm, and Zia Christina, her chickens in the garbage while we ate farina, and all the others who crowd in on me tonight while I think of my pink bedroom, cheap pink of cheap paint, and the pipes in the bathroom and the wallpaper Ma bought, how lovely it was, and even with it up, the bathroom ugly, and the linoleum in the dining room and the sofabed for Al and crowded and Molly whose husband stopped sleeping with her when she got cancer you know where and he said she wasn't a woman anymore and she cried and cried. How they crowd in on me tonight. How rich I was, though I didn't know it then.

1981

Morning in New Jersey

Morning in New Jersey. Houses
and leaning oaks.

I pull this gray day toward me,
hear the insistent pulse of earth
knocking in its arched room.

I reach to touch it. My hand finds
only brown branch and misty air.

Under my fingers, I feel a movement
so slight I am not certain it is there
and a warm center as if a volcano

were burning deep underground.

1982

Oak Place Musings

I

On my neighbor's roof, plastic butterflies
freeze in rigid postures. Rubber ducks waddle
into trimmed evergreens; plaster cats climb
siding toward peaked roofs.

Once, in a vacant Paterson lot, I caught
a butterfly; the lot seemed huge. Daisies
grew there and marigolds and red berries
which stained our fingers. We had crepe paper
whirlers in varied colors; we spun and spun.
The whirlers were an army of insects
buzzing, till tall grass and flowers blurred.

The butterfly in my hand beat its wings
in terror. My hand stained gold.
When I let it escape it flew away fast,
and then, forgetting, it dipped and swirled
so gracefully I almost stopped breathing.

II

By nine each morning, Oak Place with its neat box
houses lies still and empty. Children have vanished
into yellow camp buses, parents departed in separate cars.

The street settles into somnolence. Its lines
and angles imprison handkerchief lawns
until even the old oaks no longer seem at home.
In my yesterdays I dreamed myself out of the old city,
imagining a world just like this one,
away from strewn garbage and houses stacked close as teeth.

Today I mourn tomatoes ripening in our immigrant gardens,
the pattern of sun on walls of old brick mills,
a time when each day opened like a morning glory.
Some days when I look at my hand, I imagine
it is still stained gold.

1985

After the Children Leave Home

Slowly, we settle into the quiet house.
We almost grow accustomed to the noise
of absence, that terrible stillness
that slides along carpeted surfaces.
"The house is so quiet without them,"
you say, your voice husky with loss.

For years, we have adjusted ourselves
to their schedules, the nights of fever
and coughing, the days of car pools
and tinker toys, PTA meetings
and homework, our time together
torn by their needs.

Now facing each other across this empty
landscape, we are vulnerable
as creatures suddenly bereft of skin.
Somewhere along the way, caught in our busyness,
we lost the habit of speech,
the pathways leading to the secrets
of the heart. So we begin
slowly our grave dance, moving
through the braille of touch
into that textured country
where words are unnecessary.
Our bodies give warmth and comfort
as we struggle to reinvent the language
through which we name ourselves.

Love Poem to My Husband

From the lobby
of the Best Western Motel
in Ontario, California,
I watch the cars speed by
on the two-lane highway,
and think of you.

Yesterday, I flew across
3,000 miles of sky,
the country below
blurred by clouds,
and then to Ontario airport,
long and open like no airport
I've ever seen,
and to this motel
in the middle of honking horns
and roar of plane
motors. The farther
I move away from you,
the more you are with me.
I am cut adrift,
here alone for a week
I don't know how I'll live through.
The heat oppresses me
and the thought of you
so far away.

Here, these cars, this noise,
this sun that shimmers
on asphalt teach me more
than years in our yellow house.
I was too close to see;
only now do I learn,

without you a part of me
that flies and sings dies.

I can feel the soft, clean smell
of your skin, your hands
as you kissed me goodbye,
your eyes, dark with worry,
not wanting to let me go.

Love,
forgive my inattention,
my yearning for a freedom
I do not want.

The Morse Code of Love

On the New Jersey Turnpike, I drive
toward the Barron Art Center.
The refineries spew acrid smoke
over the houses and people.
I wonder, do those who live here
stop smelling the odor that makes me
want to hold my breath
till I've passed Elizabeth?

I get off the Turnpike,
follow signs to Route 9,
lose the exit
and drift through grimy, honky-tonk
towns lined with McDonald's and Burger King,
Goodrich Tires and Hess Gas Stations.

When I arrive at the reading, the Center
is not air-conditioned, and we are crowded
into a small room. My friend, the poet,
reads well, savoring the drama of his words.
Sometimes another friend accompanies him
on the flute, the sound plaintive and sad
in the still air. I think of Jennifer
alone in Washington and wish I had not missed
her call. I try to imagine her
sleeping in her dorm room trying
to make it lovely. I wonder if her
boyfriend has delivered the final axe stroke.

As I drive through Niagaras of rain past Rahway State Prison
and bars that are seedy and neon-lit, I look for signs
that seem to have vanished, and call out to her
in the Morse Code of love. Daughter, imagine
that I am holding you and that this loneliness, too,
can be soothed and comforted.

Uncertainties

When seen from the window
of TWA's Flight Number 171,
the clouds are thick as banks of snow.
I swear I could step out of this window
and walk thigh-deep in snow
just as the children did
in the winters
of long ago.

I remember when the ground seemed so firm
beneath my feet, when I was sure
I knew exactly where I'd be
a year from then. Today the path ahead
is like those clouds; it appears to be solid;
yet, if I were to lift the heavy door that guards us
and step outside this window,
I would meet the cavern
of empty space
into which I'd fall.

Talismans

I

Each day, Miss Elmer wore
a different flowered silk dress,
a cameo at the neck, a small
white collar. She smelled dusty
as though she had been left
too long in a closet.
Crack! went her ruler across our hands.
Crack! Crack! against small white knuckles.
"Hold out your hands," and our hands trembled.

II

Thinking of myself in second grade
and of Miss Elmer, I see,
from a world far removed from tenements
and naked bathroom pipes,
my mother's face, serious and intent,
as she pins an evil-eye horn
and scapula to my undershirt. Wearing them,
I am sure I can go out into the world
protected.

Now, when walking out of the house
each morning has become an act of courage,
I wish I could feel them there still,
breathing next to my skin.

This Shell

For Robert Bly

This shell, this delicate fan, is fluted with alternating brown and white lines curved out from the center and at the top, frail white wings, transparent as fine china. On its underside, a circle of mottled earth color, autumn leaf color, arcs over a white bowl with a tan center. I imagine the bowl holds milk and that some child might pretend it is a cup for a doll, might make a tea party with them, a circle of small shell cups, and suddenly I remember a birthday party. It is my twelfth birthday, and my friends sit around our table, laughing and pretending to be grown-up. There are no boys at this party, so the girls do not really want to be here. But, not to hurt my feelings, they have come. My mother, small and compact, bustles around us, serving our food. Without warning, my mother slaps me so hard the mark of her fingers remains on my face. I do not know what I said to provoke her anger. I only remember the party before, perfect and formed like the fluted shell; and the party after, broken, and myself, growing more transparent with each moment.

Christmas Shopping for My Mother
December, 1985

You, with your craving for order,
       with your delicate touch,
       with your small-boned hands
that keep us from harm,

I want to give you something
so beautiful it will be exactly
what you have always wanted,
something to make up for
the five and dime ornaments
you made do with
all those Paterson years.

In memory, I see you
in the old, brown rocker,
your needle moving rhythmically
in and out of sleeves
of huge army coats,
see you, long after we are in bed,
pulling basting stitches,
till a pile of thread covers your feet,

see your hands scrubbing clothes
on the tin washboard, your face intent
and lined even at thirty,
remember you ironing our clothes
to crispness under the light
of a dim bulb.

I want to give you
a diamond to make up for
the one you never had,
days sunny with leisure.

I leave Meyer Brothers's aisle,
step out into frigid December air,
knowing there is nothing I can buy for you.

I bow to your courage
and your back that was never broken
or bent, no matter what,
and bring you, instead, this poem.

1985-86

God Is Not Easy

God is not easy
like the plastic Jesus
you put on the dashboard
who glows in the dark
so you can always find him.

If he were easy,
I could slip him
in and out of a little velvet
purse whenever I wanted
him and put him back
when I didn't.

I wish he were easy
like my mother's God
who comes to her
whenever she asks
and sends her bluejays
that sing in January
so she'll know he's there.

God is
complex as the ear of the cat,
hard as the pit
in an unripened peach.

If only God would stay
in the Tabernacle, I could open
the little gold door any time
of the day or night
and there he'd be,
small and smiling,

safe as a chicken
or a goose.

Sometimes when my heart
is a dumb stone and webs
of grief catch in my eyelids,
he hands me a mountain,
alight with autumn,
or the sudden white petals
on a Japanese Cherry tree.

But God is smoke or air;
whenever I think I've caught him,
he escapes through my fingers.
I am left holding
emptiness,
a blank space
that can never be filled.

1987

55

Mrs. Sinnegan's Dogwood

I

On this morning in May,
Mrs. Sinnegan's dogwood
suddenly blossoms all white lace,
a delicate tracery
that filters light.

Each spring, I watch this tree
for the moment of silver light
when the long sleep ends and the words
that have lain dormant in darkness
rise from ashes.

II

I remember the Japanese cherry tree that bowed
just outside my window; for years
the scent of blossoms perfumed my dreams.
I see the trees, the one inextricably woven
into the years of my growing; the other
tied to middle age, a double image,
iridescent and floating.

Mrs. Sinnegan drags her chair down her back steps,
one trembling hand on her walker,
the other pulling a metal lawn chair.
She positions her chair
so she can see the tree.

At eighty her bright eyes fade to pale blue,
and her words crawl.

Yet her heart
leaps through meadows
of clover and Queen Anne's lace.

III

This year, the dogwood blooms for weeks
like a special gift.
The leaves make patterns
on the roof. The birds gather
at the feeder and then perch on the edge
of my window, singing.
One day, Mrs. Sinnegan says the tree
looks like a girl in a communion veil;
another, like a bride pulling her satin train.
Today I imagine the tree is a matron
in a flowered hat.

Arturo

I told everyone
your name was Arthur,
tried to turn you
into the imaginary father
in the three-piece suit
that I wanted instead of my own.
I changed my name to Marie,
hoping no one would notice
my face with its dark Italian eyes.

Arturo, I send you this message
from my younger self, that fool
who needed to deny
the words
(Wop! Guinea! Greaseball!)
slung like curved spears,
the anguish of sandwiches
made from spinach and oil;
the roasted peppers on homemade bread,
the rice pies of Easter.

Today, I watch you,
clean as a cherub,
your ruddy face shining,
closed by your growing deafness
in a world where my words
cannot touch you.

At eighty, you still worship
Roosevelt and J.F.K.,
read the newspaper carefully,
know with a quick shrewdness
the details of revolutions and dictators,

the cause and effect of all wars,
no matter how small.
Only your legs betray you
as you limp from pillar to pillar,
yet your convictions remain
as strong now as they were at twenty.
For the children, you carry chocolates
wrapped in gold foil
and find for them always
your crooked grin and a five-dollar bill.

I smile when I think of you.
Listen, America,
this is my father, Arturo,
and I am his daughter, Maria.
Do not call me Marie.

The Young Men in Black Leather Jackets

Today I am reminded
of the young men
who stood for hours
in front of the candy store
on 19th Street and 2nd Avenue
in Paterson, New Jersey,
the young men in black leather
jackets and tough faces,
their ducktail haircuts identical,
the young men who stared with hard
bright eyes at the girls passing by
and made comments like "Here, chickie, chickie,
c'mere, chickie," their laughter following us
down the street.

One day, as I dreamed my way through
one of the long novels I loved,
their footsteps sounded on the pavement.
The three of them walked in perfect step,
their long legs scissoring as they sang
in their loudest voices:

> *My Bonnie lies over the ocean.*
> *My Bonnie lies over the sea.*
> *My mother lies over my father's knee*
> *And that's how they got little me.*

For years, I remember their song,
the look of terrible mockery in their eyes,
their hatred of women and their need of them.
I remember that it was August. Late. Almost time
for school again. They are seventeen or eighteen;
I am thirteen.

I do not understand their song; I only know
I am ashamed as though I, and not they,
had done wrong.

Growing Up Italian

When I was a little girl,
I thought everyone was Italian,
and that was good. We visited
our aunts and uncles,
and they visited us.
The Italian language smooth
and sweet in my mouth.

In kindergarten, English words fell on me,
thick and sharp as hail. I grew silent,
the Italian word balanced on the edge
of my tongue and the English word, lost
during the first moment
of every question.

It did not take me long to learn
that dark-skinned people were greasy
and dirty. Poor children were even dirtier.
To be dark-skinned and poor was to be dirtiest of all.

Almost every day
Mr. Landgraf called Joey
a "spaghetti bender."
I knew that was bad.
I tried to hide
by folding my hands neatly
on my desk and
being a good girl.

Judy, one of the girls in my class,
had honey-blonde hair and blue eyes.
All the boys liked her. Her parents and
grandparents were born in America.

They owned a local tavern.
When Judy's mother went downtown,
she brought back coloring books and candy.
When my mother went downtown, she brought back
one small brown bag with a towel or a sheet in it.

The first day I wore my sister's hand-me-down coat,
Isabelle said, "That coat looks familiar. Don't
I recognize that coat?" I looked at the ground.

When the other children brought presents
for the teacher at Christmas, embroidered silk
handkerchiefs and "Evening in Paris" perfume,
I brought dishcloths made into a doll.

I read all the magazines that told me
why blondes have more fun,
described girls whose favorite color was blue.
I hoped for a miracle that would turn my dark skin light,
that would make me pale and blonde and beautiful.

So I looked for a man
with blond hair and blue eyes
who would blend right in,
and who'd give me blond, blue-eyed children
who would blend right in
and a name that would blend right in
and I would be melted down
to a shape and a color
that would blend right in,
till one day, I guess I was forty by then,
I woke up cursing
all those who taught me
to hate my dark, foreign self,
and I said, "Here I am –
with my olive-toned skin,

and my Italian parents,
and my old poverty,
real as a scar on my forehead,"
and all the toys we couldn't buy,
and all the words I didn't say,
all the downcast eyes
and folded hands
and remarks I didn't make,
rise up in me and explode

onto paper like firecrackers
                    like meteors
and I celebrate
              my Italian American self,
rooted in this, my country, where
all those black/brown/red/yellow
olive-skinned people
soon will raise their voices
and sing this new anthem:

Here I am
      and I'm strong
      and my skin is warm in the sun
      and my dark hair shines,

and today, I take back my name
and wave it in their faces
like a bright, red flag.

In Memory We Are Walking

In memory we are walking
single file, up Goffle Road.

We are carrying an old red blanket
and tin buckets
that clang against each other
as we move.

We have been walking for more than an hour.
At last, we stop, sit for a moment
on grass and drink the lemonade
my mother made before we left home.

Then with my mother shouting commands
like a general, we spread out the blanket
under a mulberry tree, each of us taking
a corner, my father shaking the limbs
of the tree. Huge purple fruit
fall thick and noisy as hail.

We laugh and capture mulberries
until the blanket sags with the weight.
Delicately, my mother scoops mulberries
into our buckets, gives us each
some to eat.

We walk along the brook,
watch the water rush
over rocks, and follow
the brook toward home.

I am ten years old.
I have seldom been out of Paterson.

The houses we pass,
squat, middle-class bungalows,
seem to be the houses
of the wealthy when seen through
my eyes.

On the way back, my brother is tired;
he drags behind, until my father
puts him on his shoulders. My legs hurt,
but I would not say it for the world.
I am happy. I do not know
that in the houses neighboring the park
people have watched us. They hate
our dark skin, our immigrant clothes.

My father tells us that, a few years before,
he walked all the way to Passaic and back,
following the railroad tracks
because he heard there was a job open.
He did not have five cents for the train.

When he got to Passaic, the foreman
told him there were no jobs. The workers
turned to watch him leave,
their eyes strong as hands on his back.
"You stupid Dago bastard," one called.
"Go back where you come from.
We don't want your kind here."

In the Still Photograph, Paterson, New Jersey, Circa 1950

We are standing in a backyard.
Part of a porch is visible, a lattice
heavy with roses, a small tree.
Beyond the bushes in the background,
a woman with her hand on her hip
stares at us.

My father is young. He squints
into the sun. He wears a white shirt,
a flowered tie, a pair of gabardine pants
and dress shoes. His hair is thick
and crew cut. My mother wears high-heeled
black shoes with a strap across the ankle
and nylons and a black dress
printed with large flowers,
her hair, bobbed and neat.
Her arm, bent at the elbow,
looks strong and firm.
I cannot see her expression clearly,
but I think she is smiling.
Her hand is on my sister Laura's arm,
Laura stands between them.
She is thirteen, her skin clear and beautiful.

Alex and I share a small stool
in front of the three grouped
behind us, my long hair drawn back
in a straight line. I sit
behind him. He is about seven,
slim and dressed up in imitation
of my father, except Alex wears
a bow tie. His knees look sharp

and boney through his pants,
his hands clasped together
between his knees.

Even in the standard family picture,
we do not look American.

I think of my mother's preparations:
The rough feel of the washcloth
and Lifebouy soap against my face,
the stiff, starched feel of my blouse,
the streets of Paterson, old and cracked,
the houses leaning together
like crooked teeth, the yards
that grow larger as we climb the hill,
the immigrant gardens.

We walk back home
in early evening, after the grown-ups
have espresso and anisette and
we, small jelly glasses of juice.
My brother's hand in mine, I pretend
to be grown up. Dreams
cluster around my head
like a halo, while crickets
fill the summer evening
with their shining web of song.

Connections

Some days, when the world
seems to be chasing me
with an axe and I'm driving along,
on the way home from work,
or to the post office or some other
ordinary place, I find myself
pulling into my mother's driveway
almost as though the car
decided, incredibly, to drive
toward there instead of heading
for home where the clothes wait
to be washed and the dinner cooked
and my poems wait to be placed
in clean white envelopes
and sent out to editors.
Anyway there I am, without
intending to be, knocking
on my mother's door and
she is there. She welcomes me,
smiling and criticizing,
glad to see me
even though she tells me
my hair does not look right
and why don't I wear some make up
and if she doesn't tell me,
who will? She cleans off
the already clean white table
in the basement kitchen
where she does all her cooking
(the first floor kitchen
is never used, and looks
showroom new) and takes out a cup
and pours me an espresso

without even asking and looks
in the refrigerator to see if there is anything
else that I want. She asks
about each item, warms up
some pasta and fagoli or some lentils and rice,
and sits down to talk. I marvel
at how small she is when she sits down,
her hands delicate,
with tiny bones, and her body compact.
Looking at her face, I realize,
suddenly, that she could die,
that if she were not here
for me, I would have no one
to go to for sustenance,
as I come to her, looking
for the food that satisfies
all hunger, knowing that no matter what,
she is there for me, and that I need
to have her there, as though
the world were a quaking bog
and she, the only solid place
on which to stand.

My Grandmother's Hands

I never saw them.
Once she sent a picture of herself,
skinny as a hook, her backdrop
a cobbled street and a house
of stones.
In a black dress and black stockings,
she smiles over toothless gums,
old years before she should have been,
buttoned neck to shin in heavy black.
Her eyes express an emotion
it is difficult to read.

I think of my mother's mother
and her mother's mother, traced
back from us on the thin thread of memory.
In that little mountain village,
the beds where the children
were born and the old ones died
were passed from one generation
to the next, but when my mother married,
she left her family behind. The ribbon
between herself and the past
ended with her,
though she tried to pass it on.

And my own children cannot understand
a word of the old language,
the past of the village so far
removed that they cannot find
the connection between it
and themselves, will not pass it on.
They cannot possess it,
not in the way we possessed it

in the 17th Street kitchen,
where the Italian stories and the words
fell over us like confetti.

All the years of our growing
were shaped by my mother,
the old brown rocker,
the comfort of her love
and the arms that held us
secure in that tenement kitchen,
the old stories weaving connections
between ourselves and the past,
teaching us so much about love
and the gift of self
and I wonder: Did I fail
my own children? Where
is the past I gave to them
like a gift? I have tried
to love them so that always
they will imagine that love
wrapping them, like a cashmere sweater
warm and soothing on their skin.
The skein of the past
stretches back from them to me to my mother,
the old country, the old language lost,
but in this new world, saved and cherished:
the tablecloth my grandmother made,
the dresser scarves she crocheted,
and the love she taught us to weave,
a thread of woven silk
to lead us home.

The Crow

I

The voices of the old ones follow us,
warnings in whispers,
fear fed to us in bottles
along with our milk.
The first time alone,
we stand, terrified
and perfectly still,
in the kitchen
waiting for them to come home

II

From a distance, I am awed
by the prizes you wear
like a crown.
When I meet you, your face
is the glass in which I am reflected.
In your voice, I hear a shaking so deep
I expect you to fly apart.
Though our names, changed by marriage,
are anonymous, the immigrant faces
line up in our heads. We count them,
compulsively, as if they were beads.

In our ears,
a voice,
connected to us like a cord,
whispers
you aren't really very much
you guinea, you wop,
so we struggle
to blot out the sound of the crow
who sits on our shoulder and laughs,

blot out the voice
that belittles all we do,
and drives us to be best.
My daughter she's ugly
but smart.

III

I tell you
about the reading with the poet
of the beautiful hair who keeps tossing
her head back, that glorious mane,
while I huddle in my chair
and think of having to follow her,
to get up just after she sits down.

How my insides quake
and that hair,
but I get up and turn the joke
against myself before they can.
My mother tells me I'm beautiful
but I know she means inside.

IV

You know,
I know,
we know,
who always has to be best?
We are driven women,
and we'll never escape
the voices we carry within us.

17th Street: Paterson, New Jersey

It was almost a ceremony, the welcoming of company. The aunts and uncles, the espresso pot, the espresso poured in a dark stream into the doll-sized cups set ever so delicately in their little saucers, a small sliver of lemon rind added to float near the top, then the sugar in its bowl, the spoon, midget-sized, made especially to go with those cups and saucers, and the little clink while they stirred their coffee, the men at one end of the table. Sometimes they passed out little glasses, the size of a quarter and almost one inch high, a tiny handle attached, and my father poured whisky or brandy for them, mostly the men, but sometimes the women, too. The children, sitting between the adults, were given coffee in their cups, a drop or two of coffee and lots of milk and sugar, and they listened to the stories about their parents' friends: the wayward children, the wives who were faithful or not, the men who were fools.

Listening, wide-eyed, believing, I learned more in those moments than I could in years of school about laughter and the way of opening up to others and welcoming them in, and of the magic at the heart of ordinary lives, so that ordinary things transfigured them.

Looking back, I see that ever since, I have been searching for that sweetness, the warm bread-baking aroma, the smoothness of oil cloth, its rubbery smell, the open look of my father's face, sparks flying from him in his pleasure, my mother's hand, delicate, the charm of those moments where I rested in the luminous circle of love.

April 28, 1988

Paterson: Alpha and Omega

I am twelve years old.
I am slim with new breasts
and a bra, size 32, triple a
and black slacks my mother calls dungarees,
but they're nothing like the blue jeans
the popular kids wear;
they're an inexpensive version
of those jeans and in them,
despite my new figure, I feel
awkward and uncomfortable.
I know they are the wrong kind,
and in the world of the seventh grade,
there is only one right kind.

The year I'm twelve I read
every Laura Ingalls Wilder book,
"Little House on the Prairie"
more real to me than the world
of 19th Street:
with its tilted stoop,
the factory across the street,
the girls who wear buckskin jackets
with fringe on them
in which they look like Daniel Boone.

When I think of 19th Street, I think of Ruthie
who used to walk home from PS 18
past my house.
One day, Ruthie walked with me to the top
of the Madison Ave hill.

At 6th Avenue, she turned
to head for the Projects
while I went on to the Riverside Branch
of the Library. She was one of the few white kids
in our class who lived in the Projects
and who was not Italian.
She had freckles on her nose,
arrived in PS 18 in seventh grade,
and was lonely.
In one long sentence,
like the kind of sentence that
Faulkner used, one of those sentences
that goes on for paragraphs, she told me
that she was going to leave
Paterson and the Projects
and was going to move in with her wealthy aunt
and have all the clothes she could ever want
and then everyone
would want to be her friend.
Even as she spoke, I knew
she was lying, fabricating
a story she wanted to believe
so desperately
that when she was finished,
she almost believed it herself.
I cringed for her, nodded, agreed.
After that day, she avoided
me as much as she could,
looked past me
as though I didn't exist
and though she must have graduated
with us, I don't remember seeing her again
until we are sophomores at Eastside High School.

I am in Alpha classes.
Most of my classes are on the third floor.
One day, as I am walking into the building,
I see her in the front lobby.
She is standing with a runty-looking boy
in jeans and a black-leather jacket.
His pimpled face leans toward Ruthie,
and Ruthie, her back to the wall, reaches up
to him and he kisses her, a long movie-star kiss.
Her skirt is tight and cheap-looking,
her blouse is a see-through nylon,
with her breasts sticking out of it
in obvious little points, but it's her face
I remember best. While he kisses her,
her eyes are open. Accidentally, I look
right into them. I see her cringe,
a flash of shame in her face, and then,
the hot surge of defiance. I know
that she is already lost, probably was lost
even on that day three years before
when we walked up the Madison Avenue hill
and she told the story of how she would escape
from the tightening ring of her life.

Eighth Grade

Eighth grade smells of chalk dust
mingled with Miss Richmond's sultry perfume.
The feel of our smooth wooden pen holders,
the silver nibs, the black ink in our inkwells,
the initials carved into our desks and
the bottled ink, the wooden floor,
scratched and scarred, the sun falling across it
in swatches and the dust swirling
like atoms through sunlight,
the green blackout shades, the maps
on pulleys that slide down over the board
Miss Richmond in her tight sweaters,
her gold jewelry, her high heels tapping,
tapping on the wooden floor.
A sense of life seethes below the surface,
all the rows of young people
yearning for their lives to begin.

One day Miss Richmond said,
"Today I'm going to tell you
who will go on to college,"
and she went down each row and said,
"you will and you won't and you will
and you won't."
I prayed and crossed my fingers for luck
and prayed. "Please, please, let her say yes."

When she came to me, she paused,
looked at me
a minute, and then, slowly, hesitating she said,
"You probably will."
Her hesitancy burns in my memory,
a wound that will never heal,
a taste in my mouth cruel and bitter as tin.

My Sister

When we were little, my sister
climbed trees, disappeared
after school with our cousin Philip
and the other boys
from our neighborhood.
Extroverted and practical, she leaped
into action, did not think too much.
She gloried in doing:
the tree climbed;
the tree house built;
the baseball game played.

When my sister turned twelve
she grew into a size 36D.
She walked languidly,
laughing
and joking with the other girls
outside the school,
but she came right home.

The boys who had been her friends watched her;
they waved casually and turned away,
but for a long time,
they did not look at one another.
The words for what they felt,
slipped through their fingers,
burning like sand at high noon.

Thinking About the Intricate
Pathways of the Brain

This snail shell is smooth and cool
in my hand, smooth as the slide
in the playground at the Riverside Oval,
the silver surface slippery
so that I slid to the ground in a rush
that took my breath away.
The inside shell is reached
through a curved lip
that forms a laughing or
sneering mouth,
and inside, a small protected curve,
and in the deepest
part of it, shadows.

I think if you could travel into it
deep enough, if you could take that journey
to the center, you'd discover
the witches waiting
with their chants and runes,
but if we gave them names,
they'd be able to escape,
like all the fears of which we are ashamed
and all the memories that lie
in the rabbit warrens
of the brain,
pathways that lead
to the witches with their
bags full of the past.

The self that is still
six years old is afraid
of heights
and of the older child
pushing the swing higher and
the laughter and terror caught
in our throats and the sky
washed in blue light moving, moving,
our legs reaching up
toward leafy trees and the perfect
puffy clouds of a July morning.

January 23, 1991

Columbus and the Road to Glory

In fourth grade, we chanted
"In Fourteen Hundred and Ninety-two,
Columbus sailed the ocean blue."
We recited the names of his ships,
the *Nina,* the *Pinta,* the *Santa Maria,*
and gave them back on test after test.
In our history books, Columbus was a hero,
part of the fabric of our American lives,
the lump in our throat when we heard
"The Star Spangled Banner" or
recited the "Pledge of Allegiance."

In Paterson, my father joined the Società Cilentanna
formed by those Southern Italians
spewed out of mountain villages in Campagnia, those people
that Henry Cabot Lodge called an "inferior species,"
though they were welcome in America,
cheap, unskilled labor for the jobs
no one else wanted.

My father was grateful
to get a job as a dyer's helper in a silk mill.
And when he hurt his back lifting
the heavy rolls of silk,
he became a night watchman in a school
and when he could no longer
walk the rounds ten times a night,
he got a job in a rubber factory,
gauging the pressure on steam boilers
to make sure they didn't explode.
He worked the night shift for nineteen years,

the boilers so loud he lost 90%
of the hearing in both ears.

My father, who at eighty-six still balances
my checkbook, worked for a man
who screamed at him
as though he were a fool,
but by teaching himself the basic laws of the U.S.A.,
he learned to negotiate the system
in his broken English,
spoke up for the immigrants
when they were afraid to speak,
helped them sell property in Italy
or send for their wives and children.

On Columbus Day, dressed
in his one good suit,
his shirt, starched and white,
his dark-colored, sedate tie,
appropriate for solemn occasions,
my father stood at the podium,
loving America, believing it to be
the best and most beautiful country
in the world,
a place where his children
and the children of the others
could go to school, get good jobs.
On Columbus Day,
he could forget the laughter
of the Americans who spit at him
on the street, called him
"Dago, Guinea, Wop, Gangster,
Garlic Eater, Mafioso,"
their eyes sliding sideways
when they came near

and the rules –
"No Italians need apply."

For those Italians, living
in their tenements, surviving ten hours a day
at menial jobs, Columbus Day was their day
to shine, like my father's tuba, polished
for the occasion, my father, grinning
and marching, practicing his patriotic speech.

When I see the Italians' need to cling
to Columbus as their hero, I remember
that the biggest mass lynching
in American history was of Italians
and I remember the Italians of Frankfurt, Illinois,
dragged from their houses and beaten and lynched,
and their houses burned to the ground,
and the Italians lynched in Wiltsville, Ohio,
and New Orleans and Florida
but, most of all, I remember the men at the Società,
the way they brought Columbus out once a year,
dusted him off, and presented him
to the world as their hero,
so that on that one day, they, too,
could walk tall and be proud.

And in this year of political correctness,
when I am asked to sign a petition
written by Italian American Writers
boycotting Columbus, I am angry
and I wonder: Have things changed so much for us?
Why are we always last in line, either ginzoes
in gold chains or mafiosos, found guilty
by reason of our names?

Now even this one day
set aside for Italian pride
is being ripped from our hands.

"Sta zitta, Don't make trouble!
Non far mala figura," my mother always said
but I say: Let us tell our mothers *"Sta zitta,"*
Let us tell them we don't care about *mala figura.*
Let us put the pieces of Columbus back together,
even if the cracks show, the imperfections.

Let us pick up our flawed hero,
march him through the streets of the city,
the way we carried the statue
of the Blessed Virgin at Festa.
Let us forget our mother's orders,
not to make trouble,
not to call attention to ourselves,
and in honor of my father and the men of the Società,
and in honor of my mother and the courage
and pride she taught me,
I say: No to being silent,
No to calling us names,
No to giving up Columbus,
we have a right
with our Italian American voices
to celebrate our American lives.

The Leavetaking

To my son

I thought I could buy him happiness
all wrapped up in gold foil and ribbon.
And now, when he hurls it all in my face,
when he tells me, "Leave me alone.
I don't need you anymore,"
it takes me a week to hear.

He is taking his bureau and bed,
packing his models and books
in boxes labelled John
and putting them in the attic.
I want to cry, but I am turning
his room into my study,
and I will let him go.
I will not tell him
how to spend his money
or how to organize his new life.
I will pretend not to notice
that after this move,
he will not return to this house.
He will come back only for short visits,
sleep on the new day bed in my study,
a guest in the room that has always been his.

And I will be shy with him,
as I try to replace the picture
of the child I held and comforted
with this one, of the man
whose life is cut off from my own,
connected only in subterranean ways

with the child in the past,
clutching his matchbox toys in his small fist
and building towers with plain wooden blocks,
while the remains of the past are packed
in brown cardboard boxes labelled John.

I watch him. He waves goodbye absently,
his gray eyes fixed on the new world ahead.
I remain behind, a cardboard silhouette in a doorway,
knowing all the tears in the world
cannot alter this leavetaking, necessary and final.

August 12, 1987

Out of the Window of My Classroom

Today looking at rain through a window
and brown buildings and triangles
of clipped grass, I see that nothing,
except my name, is truly mine.
All the things I thought to hold forever
the people I have loved. First my son John
moving into his life with the speed of a comet,
the distance between us larger than the space
between Mars and Venus so that I hear his voice
coming toward me from a far place,
and Jennifer, daughter of my dearest dream,
whose voice reaches toward me across phone wires,
the cord between growing thinner
with each day: like pulled taffy, it stretches
and stretches, though I know that soon it, too, will break.
Even my mother, who has always seemed so strong,
suddenly shrinks: her eyes
get smaller with each day. Blinded
by cataracts, she peers at a world
drowning in milky light, and you,
whom I thought to hold after all others
had gone, you grow stooped
and old, years before your time.

Lament for Lost Time

Tonight I wish that I could make
the years roll back for my father,
who complains, while his hands tremble,
about not being able to tie his own shoes.
He rants against his legs so weak
and nearly useless, his swollen feet.
His eyes, hooded like a bird's, are feverish,
"stonati," like someone
who is being battered.
His face has a slash of color
across too-white skin.
In the chair next to him,
my mother lies curled,
holding a hot water bottle
wrapped in flannel, her face
white and dry as a communion wafer.
"Pray I'll be O.K.,"
she says, "or what will happen?"
She means what will happen
to your father? But when she sees
my panic, she shakes the fear
from her eyes and rises to comfort me.

Home Movies

In the old movie, 1957, we are dancing.
Our new house seems so beautiful.
The street, tree-lined and fragrant,
looks like a country lane,
and outside our bedroom window,
the Japanese cherry tree blooms.
We have just moved from
the 19th Street tenement
with its cement back yard,
small as a handkerchief.

I see myself lying full length
on the sofabed in the cellar.
I read in Seventeen magazine
about a young woman who lived
in a "modest" bungalow.
In the picture I see it is exactly like our house,
with its screened-in front porch,
its boxy living room and dining room.
its two bedrooms with room enough in them
for a double bed
and a small dresser.

How our eyes change as we grow older.
The world around us blurs,
but the world that lives in our minds
grows sharper, the picture clear
and focused. We notice details
we had missed before.

Looking back, I see my mother.
She is young, shapely, sensuous.
She dances with my brother.
She is laughing.
My sister twirls around me.
My brother chases us, saying,
"Look! There's Cletus! Let's get him,"
picking an imaginary flea out of air.

Watching the film unwind,
I feel time rushing past
like a waterfall.
The people in the movie
seem so far from us,
their clothes awkward,
out of style,
their faces untouched.

Generations

Every day I'd read to John from those small books
I'd get at the supermarket
or the cloth books I'd buy at toy stores,
and I remember Dennis reading the Wizard of Oz books to him,
but even when he still fit in the wicker clothes basket,
he'd rest in there and read a book,
his large, solemn gray eyes
absorbed in the print,
the page turning rapidly under his hand,
and he, able to tell the story
of what he'd read, almost word for word.
He liked to have us read to him,
charmed by the rhythm of the spoken word,
though even at four he could have read it faster himself,
and I think of him today,
singing chorus after chorus of "Old MacDonald Had a Farm"
because his daughter stops crying
when she hears his voice singing that song,
her large solemn eyes fixed on him,
her face, with that attentive, listening look,
her intelligence evident even at six months.
I think of my son, his daughter, the years ahead,
Caroline snuggled into the crook of his arm
and him reading to her, patiently,
though he is impatient with all else
and easily bored,
and she, loving the sound of his voice,
his arm curving around her,
his hands on her fiery hair.

Song for Caroline

Caroline, Caroline Paige,
grand-daughter,
I treasure your curious stare,
your sturdy pushing legs.
I watch your mother's face
when she holds you,
lit from within as I was
when I held your father,
that Johnson's baby powder scent,
the warm smooth feel of your skin
against my mouth,
and for one moment,
sliding back in time,
I am young again
and you are my child.

In 1965 in that Rutgers apartment,
I sat through the long, hacking night,
holding your father
and rocking into dawn light.
How warm he was in my arms,
how sure I was I would keep him forever.
Now I hold you,
the child I held so long ago
vanished:
Little flower,
little chirping bird,
you watch the world
through big, solemn eyes
drinking everything in,
storing it up
the seriousness of it all,
and you, your sudden smile

when you look at your father
as though all the glory
in the universe
were gathered in his hands.

Caroline, Caroline Paige,
Granddaughter,
today when I hold you,
you burrow into the curve
of my neck, and I wonder
when you are older
will you come to me
with your secrets
and your sorrows?
Will we become friends
a little while
before you rush into your life?
Already you are trying to walk,
your legs, too delicate to hold
your slender body,
want to walk anyway,
your feet moving through air,
practicing the motion
that will take you away.

We gather in a circle around you,
as if you were a fire and we, needing
your warmth against the chill.
Blue as pansies, as violets, your eyes
fix on each of us in turn,
your father, mother, grandfather and me.
We are awed by you, your copper hair,
your impish mouth, your legs,
so strong and wirey, and you,
and all of us, so pleased with you.
We smile at you,

this blessing, this magic charm,
this energy which crackles
in the room, so new, so new.

Paradise Motel

I wait in the Paradise Motel in this small Vermont town brimming with gray early morning light. I am waiting for the woman who has been assigned by this college to pick me up, though I'd rather eat breakfast alone. I realize I'm hungry and begin to get annoyed that she can't get herself here on time. When she arrives, we are awkward with each other. Her pants are black and white checked. They are badly wrinkled and her blouse appears tossed on. She wears a black sweater that covers her rear end. Her hair is frazzled into ringlets; it looks burned, and hangs in curled strings around her face and down her back. I try to carry on a conversation, try to find some common ground on which we can rest.

After we sit down in the Cozy Kettle Cafe and order breakfast, my attempts at conversation begin to break the uncomfortable stiffness between us. She mentions some of my poems, says how much they remind her of her mother. Then she spills out words about her life, her boyfriend whom she met on the street. She and her friend were walking down main street, she says, and she saw him pass and he said, "Hello: How are you doing tonight?" She answered and they started talking and they went to the park and sat there till 3 A.M. She's been dating him ever since. He works in a factory that makes coat hangers. He lived with a woman and has an eight-year-old son. They weren't getting along, she says, and he wanted to break up with her, but she trapped him by getting pregnant. He left her when she was eight months pregnant. "I love him," this girl says. "He makes me feel good about myself. He's the only one. We are going to get married." I say, "You are very young, try to be very sure," knowing that she will not hear. Thinking: a blue collar worker in a country where manufacturing is dying. Thinking: poor girl, poor girl. Thinking: he left his girl when she was eight months pregnant. "See," she says, "I have this hair on my chin, a lot of hair and a moustache. I've always been conscious of it, thought people would mind, but he doesn't. See, he doesn't. He shaves the hair on my chin for me." Her eyes have darkened and softened. They are now blue/green and her face, with that soft light, almost beautiful.

I am moved by seeing how much she needs to be loved, enough to blind herself to his flaws–the warning signals: his mother who lives in a filthy trailer and has piles of old junk in the yard; the deserted girlfriend, the custody battle, the dead end job. "I know I'm too fat," she says, " but I hate exercise. My mother says I have childbearing hips." "I am the decision maker," she says, "I cook and clean for him now. It's like having a baby. He needs me to take care of him."

I tell her about myself when I was her age. How shy and awkward I was, how I saw myself as ugly and fat. "You'll be surprised," I say, "how much more beautiful you'll appear when you look back at pictures in fifteen years. You won't believe it."

The long baggy sweater she wears is designed to cover her body, which, when she stands, I see is full-breasted and curvacious. In different clothes, with her hair clean and straight and falling free, her face without the closed, clod-like expression, her face, open and soft, her eyes shining, as they are now, she would be striking and beautiful. I can feel that even she knows she's marrying to keep from facing her life, running into marriage as a refuge where she can say she is married, loved, where she can feel beautiful. I hope that she cannot see my fear for her, or the pity that floods over me. She leaves me at the hotel where I will wait for the artsy student who will pick me up to take me to the train. "I'm glad you talked to me," she says. "I feel better about myself. I hope you'll come back soon." Her eyes look bruised, dark-circled, and in the parking lot, surrounded by imposing mountains and drowning in gray light, I hug her. "Good luck," I say. Her eyes fill with tears. "Yes," she says. "Yes."

Requiem for a Four-Year-Old

Mark Warner was four years old
when he died in a Paterson slum. These days
even the people in his old neighborhood
can't remember his name.
"All I know is a little boy died here.
Nobody don't talk about it."
The words are spoken casually by a tall, slender woman
with orange-red nail polish. She gives her name
only as "Tee." No last name. On this block
of Broadway in Paterson, where used crack vials
are scattered at the curb and winos
hang out all day outside a liquor store,
people don't give their full names,
Tee is nineteen. She lives in apartment 6,
the same apartment where Mark Warner lived and died.
Standing on the rickety front stoop under a broken window,
Tee says: "Everybody here now wasn't here then."

"Sometimes I just give him a couple of slaps,"
Michael Thomas, Mark's stepfather says.
"But this time I hit him a while."
In the color pictures of Mark Warner,
Mark's lower lip is split
and large purple bruises distort most of his face
and body.
Four round scars,
old cigarette burns, mark his buttocks.
The coroner believes the welts on his back
are from a whipping with a belt or a wire loop.
Assistant Passaic County Prosecutor,
Marilyn Zdobinski, shakes her head in disgust.

"These are the crimes
that people do not think happen,"
Zdobinski says.
"But people beat kids every day."

Last week, Mark's twenty-one-year-old mother,
Alvira Warner Thomas, stood silently
in an empty Passaic County Courtroom;
She was sentenced to four years probation
and ordered to seek counseling.
Michael Thomas was sentenced to ten years
without parole. "He is very depressed,"
his lawyer says.

From an article in The Herald & News
Paterson, N. J., February 13, 1988

In Falling Light, Paterson

In falling light, Paterson sky
is an incredible blue so bright
and deep it seems painted on even as it slides
toward pale pink against the ochre brick
mills. I drive past the rococo arches
of the Church painted in lavender and gray,
drive down to Oliver and then, into Mill,
past Federici's green and decaying Dublin Spring sculpture
and onto Route 80 where the stars
thicken into clusters in the blazing sky
and the lights of the city float in a sea
of space. The weight
of the day lifts, light as a gauze
shawl, off my shoulders, all
heaviness falling away before the
dizzying panorama, luminous
and vast.

March 27, 1988

Ma, Who Told Me You Forgot How to Cry

Soothsayer,
healer,
tale-teller,
there was nothing you could not do.

In your basement kitchen,
with the cracked brown and yellow tiles,
the sink on metal legs,
the big iron stove with its pots simmering,
the old Kelvinator from 1950,
the metal kitchen table and plastic chairs,
I'd watch you roll out dough for pastichelle.
"Be quiet," you'd say,
and work at super speed.

Today, when we walk into your hospital room,
you do not speak of your illness,
do not mention the doctor
who tells you bluntly,
"You have three months, at most, to live."

Your shrewd, sharp eyes watch us,
but you do not cry.

Soothsayer,
healer,
tale-teller,
always ready with a laugh and a story,
ready to offer coffee, cakes,
advice at your oval kitchen table,
your chair pulled close and your hands
always full.

We are like little children gathered
around your bed. Al, with his doctor's bag
full of tricks and medicine,
Laura, in her nurse's uniform,
her hands twisting, and me,
my head full of words
that here, in this antiseptic room,
are no use, no use at all.

We wait for you
to get up out of that bed,
to start bossing us around,
the way you always did.
Tell us a story
with a happy ending,
one in which the oil
of Santo Rocco that you put on
your swollen belly each night
works its elusive miracle.

Soothsayer,
healer,
tale-teller,
there was nothing you could not do.
Tell us again how the bluebirds
came to sing at your window
that January, when Al was so sick
all the doctors said he'd die.

But I Always Got Away

My mother dreams that two people,
one a bald-headed man, have grabbed her.
They try to push her into a small windowless room.
They will never let her out.

"No! No!" she screams at them,
lifts up two baseball bats
which miraculously appear in her hands,
and beats them on the head, very hard,
"but not enough to kill them," she assures us,
"just enough to knock them out."

"I escape," she says, "and leave them
behind me on the floor, their mouths
open." She demonstrates, opening her mouth
wide, the white line around her lips clear,
her face pale as white flour.

"You have three months, at most, to live,"
the doctor tells her, but it is one month already,
and she is beginning to get up, beginning to hope.
"I got away," she laughs and for a moment,
we are drawn into her belief. "I had the same dream
three times, but I always got away."

Ma, I Think of You Waiting

Each day for the health aide
who arrives at your house at 7 A.M. and leaves
again at 10 A.M. In the afternoon,
sometimes Orlando visits
and then at six, Al arrives.
By 6:30 P.M., you begin to wait
for me. By the time I arrive
at eight, you are leaning forward
in your chair; you are restless.
"Are you in pain?" I ask.
"No, just uncomfortable," you say.
You want to go to bed, gear up
to get out of your chair,
and are breathing hard after walking
five feet to your bed.
I help you undress, lift your clothes
over your head. You close your eyes,
your face pale and strained.
"I'm too much trouble for you kids,"
you say. I protest, stroking
your hand that each day loses
more flesh. You move over
onto your side, then onto your
back, move your legs, and then, back
onto your side again. "I'm just
not comfortable," you say. "nervous.
I don't know why."
Al says, "I hope she'll live till the new year"
but I tell Laura, "I don't know.
She seems so weak."

After I have given you your pills,
warmed your milk, given Dad
his cocoa and helped him
into bed, I get ready to leave you.
The last thing I see before I walk
out the door is your face in profile,
your nose sharper than I remembered
the bones of your skull prominent
your lips moving in prayer.

Visiting My Mother

Last night, I visited my mother and all the lies I've been telling myself about how this medicine will work and how she's going to get better are lies, and part of me knows it and the other part does not want to believe it. Watching her I see her arm is thin and that she takes two sips of lemonade after saying how thirsty she is, and then says she doesn't want anymore.

Laura has just given her Demerol and as it takes effect, she perks up. She has dark brown smudges under her eyes and her face is hollowed out. She has taken out her teeth, though she has always boasted that she never takes them out, and she tells us stories non-stop, the past filled with details she has never told us before.

When I was born, she tell us, my father walked down to the grocery store on Fourth Avenue to call the doctor. Meanwhile, she looked down and there I was, my head and shoulders emerging. "What a surprise," she says. For a moment, she is so lucid, her eyes shining, that we forget how weak she was just a few minutes ago.

When Alessandro was born, she was in the hospital in a basement delivery room and all the women were being taken in to give birth but no one came to get her. She screamed until she got the attention of a young intern who delivered the baby. The doctor never arrived. Alex had a head full of black hair when he was born. She smiles and says, "I took that young doctor's hand and said, 'Thank you. You are so good.' I wonder what happened to him? Maybe he's dead. Well, God bless him, if he's not dead."

"You know," she muses, "when you were little babies, they had a nurse who took care of you. I brought you to the school and she was there and she weighed you and measured you and gave you your shots. She had this little book that she wrote in the weight and height and which shots and then, she'd put in a gold star if the baby was well and had grown. I kept that book. Used to take it out and look at it. So nice. All those gold stars. I had it a little while ago. It was nice," she says and laughs.

Grief

It's more than three months since my mother died, and I realize how grief comes to us over and over, how it catches us unawares, how it is the small things that make us remember, the dented pot in my mother's pantry, the sad, threadbare towels, the unused nightgowns folded neatly in her bureau.

Sometimes, on the way to work, coming down River Street arching under the railroad bridge just past Our Lady of Lourdes, I remember my mother. I am driving and crying, wanting her here with me now, and I think of the times I did not call her, the times I was annoyed that she called me every day, and would give anything now to have her call me, to have her be there when I climb the stairs to her kitchen, to find there, not Irena, the Polish lady who stays with my father because he cannot be left alone, but my mother, busy and strong as she once was, energy radiating off her, her spirit courageous and indomitable so I think she can't be dead, she can't be dead, not when I still need her, and I think of how she told me she was going to have cataract surgery. We are sitting at her kitchen table the week before her operation, and we are talking about some other things, and suddenly, I say, "So when are you leaving, Ma?" "Leaving?" she says, and laughs, we both laugh, but we are both afraid, superstitious that this slip of my tongue, this question I didn't know I was going to ask, means she is going to die, but I shrug off this dire premonition, slap away the insistent voice in my head, though I should know better by now, know that I ignore the voice at my peril, and that my mother and I share this instinctive knowledge of the future that floats around us thin as veils, invisible to all eyes but ours. When she was dying, when she died and came back, she told us about the garden where her mother and sisters walked, the beautiful garden, peaceful and calm, where she sees her mother and sisters, bathed in light that transforms them to creatures magnificent in their beauty, and she says they were there and walked together, and then she turns to me, and says, "you were there, too." I think that maybe in this, too, she was right, that maybe I am going to die soon, but I tell myself no, no, I can't die yet, I have so much more I want to do, and I think of holding my niece Debbie's baby, his head resting on my chest, and her father saying how much Mom would have loved seeing him, this bruiser of a boy, this child with Debbie's mouth and the shoulders of a football player and his huge beautiful eyes who so reminds me of Debbie as a baby. How my mother would have smiled at him, laughed with us when he snored, been happy to see us all there together in Laura's kitchen, our eyes filling with grief over our loss of her.

Heritage

I'm like those Russian peasant dolls
made of lacquered wood where the larger dolls open
to reveal smaller dolls, until finally
the smallest doll of all stands, unseamed and solid.
When you open me up: my mother, her mother,
my daughter, my son's daughter. It could go on for ever,
the way I carry them inside me.
Only their voices emerge, and when
I speak to my daughter,
I hear their words tangled in my own.

Ma, when you died, I thought I'd lost you forever;
grief washes over me
when I pass your barren garden and remember
the tomatoes that grew so wildly while you
watched from the bedroom where you were dying;
or when I walk into your basement kitchen
and see that it is grimy with neglect;
or when I see Dad sitting in the big recliner,
his legs covered by a blanket you crocheted
and a picture of you propped up
on the table next to him,
but when I open myself
you are still there inside me and I am safe,
even though I cannot drive to your house
or sit down while you pour me an espresso.
This is the way it is with me –
you are nested inside me,
your voice a whisper that grows clearer
with each day.

On Reading Susan Toth's *Blooming*

Wind pointers twirl through past
summers in the 17thStreet garden,
turned earth, blacker than coal in the cellar,
smell of earth, tart and cool as
the lemonade we made
in a big glass pitcher,
lemon halves whirling
like snow in a paperweight.

Once I held one of those crystal weights in my hand.
How I loved the snow
falling softly over the perfect village and people,
the white New England Church, the small,
winding road and all of it, protected
by a glass, the way the past is for me,
boundaried and safe,
a place where I am held by hands
that love me and that I trust
never to let go.

Where I Come From

This twig, bent into a miniature bow, is cracked and peeling in spots, its bark almost silver with black dots, and in the peeled spots, the wood tan and white. Rough to the touch, it is nobby with black knots shaped like flowers or lips, but the ends are jaggedly torn, as though a careless hand snapped the twig from the tree.

I think of my mother, the doctor who says she is dying, but she hangs on to life, her body growing smaller with each day, her eyes, round and black. We sit together on the edge of her bed; her legs don't touch the floor. We look at pictures that she saved in a plastic folder; her sister, Giuseppina, who died in childbirth more than sixty years ago; her mother, spare and slim as a needle and dressed all in black, her hair pulled back in a knot at the nape of her neck, her sister, Lena, at fifty, squat and shapeless from childbearing, her face round, her skin clear and smooth, though she looks seventy in her loose black dress and black old lady shoes.

"So many stories I could tell," my mother says, "so many," and she tells us stories we had not heard before, as though her life, in all its nobbiness, bent like this twig, arched and beautiful, is being torn away. She peels at the crusty bark that has made her always the sturdy one, the one we all came to for help, and now, the wood beneath revealed, tan and clean. Her hand reaches out toward me, and when I take it and hold it in mine, it feels so light, her bones so delicate, I am surprised when it does not disappear.

THINGS MY MOTHER TOLD ME

1999

Learning Grace

"When you do something with your hands," my mother said, "you have to put your love into it, and then, it will be sacred. See?" She kneaded the bread dough, turned it over and over in her hands until her hands and the dough did their own special dance. Then she placed the dough back in its bowl, covered it with the bleached white kitchen towels she made, and left it to rise. When the towel was a hill curving high above the rim of the bowl, she lifted the dough onto the floured bread board, rolled it and shaped it into huge round loaves and long ones and, at Easter, she braided it into special shapes and baked whole eggs in it in set patterns she learned when she was a girl in San Mauro from her own mother. With the dough, she made crosses over the eggs and painted egg yolks over the surfaces of the loaves; then whispered a prayer over each and carefully slid them into the oven where they filled the house with the satisfying aroma of baking bread. When she took the loaves out of the oven, she smiled and broke off a piece of one loaf for us to eat with butter. Later, when she brought the bread to the table, it was a ceremony, the way she carried it in, holding a beautiful braided bread out to us, its surface glowing brown gold, the tender way she laid it in the center of the table, the way she made the sign of the cross over the loaf before she cut into it, this sustenance, this beauty, this grace she taught us to pass on.

I Dream of My Grandmother
and Great Grandmother

I imagine them walking down rocky paths
toward me, strong, Italian women returning
at dusk from fields where they worked all day
on farms built like steps up the sides
of steep mountains, graceful women carrying water
in terra cotta jugs on their heads.

What I know of these women, whom I never met,
I know from my mother, a few pictures
of my grandmother, standing at the doorway
of the fieldstone house in San Mauro,
the stories my mother told of them,

but I know them most of all from watching
my mother, her strong arms lifting sheets
out of the cold water in the wringer washer,
or from the way she stepped back,
wiping her hands on her homemade floursack apron,
and admired her jars of canned peaches
that glowed like amber in the dim cellar light.

I see those women in my mother
as she worked, grinning and happy,
in her garden that spilled its bounty into her arms.
She gave away baskets of peppers,
lettuce, eggplant, gave away bowls of pasta,
meatballs, zeppoli, loaves of homemade bread.
"It was a miracle," she said.
"The more I gave away, the more I had to give."

Now I see her in my daughter,
that same unending energy,
that quick mind,
that hand, open and extended to the world.
When I watch my daughter clean the kitchen counter,
watch her turn, laughing,

I remember my mother as she lay dying,
how she said of my daughter, "That Jennifer,
she's all the treasure you'll ever need."

I turn now, as my daughter turns,
and see my mother walking toward us
down crooked mountain paths,
behind her, all those women
dressed in black.

My Son Tells Me Not to
Wear My Poets Clothes

My son tells me not to wear my poet's clothes. "They're weird," he says. He wants me to look like a mail-order catalogue grandmother, with preppy cardigan and corduroy skirt, wear the kind of clothes that would have been all wrong for me even at twenty. I love thin, flowery dresses that float around me when I walk, long, colorful scarves with fringe on them. My son does not say it out loud, but I know he thinks I'm the wrong kind of mother, that I should act my age, give up poetry because it's strange for me to be running off to all those poetry readings and giving workshops and working so many hours a week at my job. Sometimes I think we should trade places. He could be the staid, conservative grandmother and I the recalcitrant son. When we talk on the phone, I hear how he shoulders the responsibilities of his life, wife, children, house, and job. "John," I say, "you're only thirty-one. Give yourself a break." I hear him sigh, that expelled breath fraught with meaning, the sound I make when I am anxious or bored. I am saddened when I hear it coming from him over the wires across all that distance, not only the landscape that separates us, but the language that fails us. I cannot find a way to make him understand that I love him, this son who needs to be far away from me so that it's as though I am chasing him down a path but he's always faster than me. I see him sitting with his son Jackson in his arms, Jackson who looks just like John did at two, I see the way they lean together, my grandson so relaxed and trusting, his ear pressed to his father's heart.

My Lucky Dress

Ever since I was a little girl, I thought that I had lucky clothes and unlucky ones. When I wore the lucky clothes good things happened: I won a prize in school, a teacher praised my work, I got an A, a boy I liked talked to me. When I wore the unlucky clothes, something bad happened. If I wore a certain blouse once, and that was the day that the girls in seventh grade excluded me from their club or I didn't know an answer to a question, then I was afraid to wear that blouse again. I'd like to say I've outgrown my superstitions, but I haven't. I still have "lucky" clothes and "unlucky" ones, so I give a lot of clothes away to the Salvation Army, and I've come to believe in my instincts, since like my mother before me, I can sense immediately when I am near a person who is mean-spirited or vengeful or jealous. Once, when we went to see a house we were thinking of buying, my mother came with us to see it and, as soon as she entered the front hall, my mother became very agitated saying, "Let's get out, let's get out, this house has evil spirits in it." We thought she had lost her mind and laughed at her, but later found out that three people had been murdered in that house, so when she had one of her moments, we were inclined to listen rather than to laugh. I guess you could say it's the peasant in me, this belief that I can tell when something is about to happen or know that a particular friend will call me two minutes before the phone rings, but I have learned to listen to the voice that whispers inside me. If I don't, I always regret it. So now, if you see me wearing a long black dress and a pink and green scarf with fringe on it and a jacket with marquasite pins on it from a thrift store, you'll know I wear this outfit a lot because it is my lucky dress. I suppose people are sick of seeing me in it at poetry readings but I still need to wear it, a talisman that will ward off all the malevolent spirits that hover in the room around us, especially at the moments when we want so much to be brilliant and charming and loved.

Signs

On the telephone answering machine
my mothers voice calls: "Where are you?
Eh, she ran away," she says in Italian
and hangs up.

It is ten o'clock, too late to call her back.
She must already be in her two flannel nightgowns,
her woolen socks, her hand-crocheted blankets
and clean, clean sheets tucked up to her chin.

The headboard of her maple bed shines with polish,
her bureau with its big mirror reflects her statue
of the Blessed Virgin and the votive candle that burns
and flickers in darkness and is always lit.

In her hand, my mother holds her rosary;
around her neck, she wears medals imprinted
with the face of Saint Anthony, a small gold evil eye horn,
a scapula pinned to her nightgown.

At each bead of her rosary, she recites a prayer,
a monotonous litany in Italian. When she has finished
praying, she hangs her rosary on the bedpost,
adjusts her hot water bottle and sleeps.

Sometimes, if something is bothering her,
even her prayers do not help,
and she dreams vivid dreams that foretell the future,
her own mother who comes to sit on her bed
the night before she dies, her dead sister
who appeared to her and whispers warnings,

dreams full of portents and signs:
plane rides that should not be taken,
people who mean us harm.

When we were children, we mocked her,
but, over the years she is so often right,
we have come to see her as powerful,
a person whose inner eye sees clearly
through all the walls of time.

My dreams, too, are vivid,
warn of impending doom,
tell me to call one of my children
at the exact moment when they need to talk
or are filled with longing.

I call my daughter, reach out
toward her with my mind
and try to sense her happiness
or sadness, judge the temperature

of her heart. She is ambivalent
toward me, wants to love me
but not love me too much.
I need to check on her,

to make sure she's not sad,
does not need help, as I checked
her forehead for fever
when she was a little girl

in a white canopy bed,
and I touched her face,
smoothed back
her beautiful hair.

Brushing My Mother's Hair

My mother is sitting up in bed,
while I straighten her covers.
If she were stronger, she would complain
that I am not smoothing the sheets
the right way, but now she is so grateful
to have me there that her eyes follow me.

Laura has given her Demerol, and has gone home.
The medicine kicks in and she perks up,
though her face still has a yellow tinge to it.
"My hair," she whispers, "my hair is messy."

She used to brush my hair when I was little.
She believed in neatness so it didn't matter
how I howled when she pulled the brush
through my thick, wiry curls.

Her hair, once as thick and wild as mine,
now is so thin and dull, the brush slides
through it easily. She sighs and relaxes.
I stand behind her so she cannot see
the way my mouth trembles.

My mother closes her eyes
and leans against me. I hold her.
She smiles, and then she picks herself up,
and says, "I'm too much trouble for you."

Singing to My Mother

I sit on my mother's bed and sing a lullaby.
"Rockabye baby," I whisper, half song, half chant,
remembering when I sat like this
on the children's beds and sang them to sleep,
only my mother is seventy-eight
and gravely ill and frightened.

Earlier today I made some *pasta e fagioli*
and my father was very happy,
after Meals-on-Wheels
and the old chickens he claims
they saved to give to all the old
people in Hawthorne.

She opens her mouth.
I spoon in food.
For the first time in many days she seems hungry
and eats a bowl and a half of *pasta e fagioli,*
her mouth opening greedily, her hand shaking.

After forty choruses of "Rockabye Baby,"
I run out of steam, and resort to
"Amazing grace, how sweet the sound,
I once was lost, and now am found."

I love that hymn, but those are the only lines I remember
since I was raised as a Catholic, and I don't know any
Protestant hymns,
and then I sing, "Away in a manger, no crib for a bed,
the little Lord Jesus lay down his sweet head."
She is holding my hand. I watch her eyes close.

Her breathing deepens. I whisper, "I guess you're asleep now."
Her eyes open and she says, "No, I'm not,"
and she tightens her grip on my hand,
as though by holding me, she could keep herself rooted
to the ground.

My Mother's Garden II

Everyday on the way to the college,
I pass the greenhouse
on the corner of River and First,
but today, after a long hibernation,
bags of fertilizer frozen in the lot,
cans and pots piled in a corner,
the garden center sprouts
row upon row of spring flowers,
daffodils yellow as butter,
the red flare of geraniums,

and I remember that last May
I went to the greenhouse with Mom.
We did not know she was sick.
I see now that she must have been going
on pure strength of will.

She has on the tan London Fog raincoat,
I bought for her at the Mission
and she is brusque with the young boys
who carry the plants to the cars.
She chooses the best plants, selects the
big boy early tomatoes
and the later growing variety;
she haggels over price,
but is pleased to have them.

The next time I go to her house,
I find the tomatoes planted in neat rows.
That next week we found out
she was gravely ill,
but all that summer
tomato plants blossomed and bore fruit,

though no one cared for the plants,
and the weeds grew around them.

The tomatoes almost jumped off the vine
while my mother watched them
from her bedroom window,
happy when she saw basket after basket
of tomatoes carried inside.
I wonder if she thought the tomatoes were a sign,
a message that she'd beat this illness
and get up to work again in her beloved garden,
her hands deep in the black earth,

but, of course, nothing happened,
except she got worse and worse
while the tomato plants flourished
Jennifer and I took turns pulling weeds,
and sitting near my mother's bed.
The tomatoes were like the last breath
leaving her body,
and when the plants were dying,
the last tomatoes picked,
she let go, the tremor of death
almost unnoticeable as she vanished from her body,
the garden more like a jungle than anything,
a reminder that hurt like a rotten tooth.

I remember Gillette who came to take care of my mother
on what turned out to be the last night of her life.
I had been there for days
and Gillette came at four so I could go home for awhile,
but Mom called me back,
made me sit near her bed,
said, "Go home now," held my hand.
Not two hours later, Gillette called,
said Mom was really sick.

She didn't know what to do.
I rushed over there
and Mom began vomiting
huge clots of blood.

Picture the scene: the hospital bed,
my mother shrunk to the size of a doll,
except for her huge belly,
her weak horrified head,
me trying to help;
calling Laura to come over.
She gave my mother a shot to stop the vomiting,
while Gillette did her laundry

and raised her voice
in cheerful song, the song
of a woman content.

Mothers and Daughters

All my life people have expected me to be strong,
to carry them like sacks on my back,
to juggle several lives in my hands
without dropping anything. "Amazing,"
they said, "How do you manage?"
and I kept on going.
Only my mother was stronger than me,
who always thought of myself as weak
and small by comparison,
until she died
and I had to step into her shoes
and was shocked to find how well they fit me.

Tonight, driving home from my father's house,
I realize that only my daughter let's me lean on her,
so when she walks into the house, it is as though she carries
a bright light with her, and I can feel my straight spine
relaxing, the tension leaving my body
so quickly I imagine I can hear it,
the way I can hear air being let out of a tire.

When I know she's coming home, all day I am happy
thinking of her sharp wit, her laugh,
the way we share so much.

My Son, That Gray-Eyed Dreamer

When I speak to my son,
it is as though we are speaking under water.

Sometimes I am afraid
that if I were walking down the street
and he were to come toward me,
I would not recognize him.

My son, that gray-eyed dreamer,
I think of him every day.
He is too far
to ever come back.

I sit in my car,
my keys in my hand,
and feel our separateness
wash down my face,
an ocean of salt on my tongue.

Passing It On

This Easter we don't really need the second table or the extra chairs carried up from the basement: my son, his wife, their two children in Virginia; my daughter, with her husband's family in Cape Cod; my father in a wheelchair and unable to sit at the table; my mother three years dead. I invite my neighbors; still there are empty chairs. My brother sits in the living room all through dinner; he has to have special food that his wife cooks for him before they leave home. He is staring at the white wall, perhaps missing one of his own sons. On an earlier Easter, I remember my Italian mother, looking vibrant and strong, cooking for all of us, seventeen of us gathered around her table, as we had gathered each Sunday and holiday in all the years while our own children grew. My father made a speech, sitting in his black rocker, his metal cane on the chair near him. His hands trembled so much the paper rattled. "Next Easter," he said in his Italian version of English, "I hope we will be together, but if something happens keep the family strong." I looked over at my mother. Her small, compact body radiated heat, and we gathered around her. By October she was dead.

After dinner, I call my son. He says they haven't eaten yet. "No company?" I ask. My son, who probably could have been a hermit, tells me we make too much noise. He has been absent for so long, I'm not sure if I miss him or only the idea of him. I wish he sounded happy rather than just tired. My four-year-old granddaughter asks to speak to me on the phone. She tells me riddles. We talk about when they will visit. "I'll bring my pocketbook," she says seriously. "I can't wait to see you, Caroline." I say. "Me too, Grandma." Then she whispers, "My momma says I'm too loud." "That's O.K., I'm loud too. When you come to my house, we'll be loud together."

As my mother said to me thirty years ago, "You don't know yet. Wait." I'd like to say the same thing to my son, but I don't. I want to tell her, "Ma, we're Americans now and look at all we've lost." She walks toward me and places a loaf of her braided Easter bread in my hands. *"Tesoro,"* she says, "give the bread to Caroline," and then she strokes my cheek with her hand.

Papa, Where Were You?

In pictures of myself when I was growing up,
I cannot find you. I search through a catalog
of memories, old pictures, frayed and yellowed.
You are not there. Papa, where were you
while Mamma kept our kitchen warm, covered up
your absence so it was years before we realized
that you were rarely home?

I remember you with your friends
under Zia Rosa's grape arbor,
playing cards with the other men,
wine in short glasses before you,
peach slices gleaming in the red wine.

I remember you, talking politics with your friends,
you, marching in the Columbus Day Parade,
you, playing the tuba in the Italian band.
All the images are of me watching you
from a distance. You rotate shifts
in the silk mill so most days you are leaving
for work or sleeping when we come home.

It is Mamma I go to when I am hurt
or crying, Mamma who listens
to my stories, Mamma who is always there.

It is only now that I remember the small moments
that spoke your love, when you could not;
the times you drove miles out of your way
to pick me up, so I wouldn't have to take the bus;
the chocolates you left in my desk drawer;
the bags of dark, sweet cherries you brought to me
every day of that first summer of my marriage;

the money you were always ready to give;
the year you took care of my daughter
so I could teach; the long hours you worked
tending a boiler or pushing a broom
to give me a life better and easier than yours.

Tonight, I find you in the brown mechanical chair from
    Medicare;
at eighty-nine, your mind still sharp and quick, you are caught
in that little house, where you move with excruciating slowness
behind your walker. All your friends are long gone or dead.
Even Mamma is only a picture propped against a tissue box
on the table next to your bed. You still want to win a million
in the lottery so you can give it to us, want to die
because you're afraid you're causing us too much trouble.
You talk politics as shrewdly as you did when you were young.

I try to visit you every day. Having found
you at last, after all my years of not seeing you,
I don't want to miss one moment sitting near you
in your hot little parlor, seeing your eyes light up
when you see me enter, telling me stories of your past,
describing the People's Revolution you think America needs.
You glance sideways at me, your nose hooked
and prominent. You smile and your face regains
the handsomeness it had when you were young.

When I was a child, you were a shadowy presence;
with each year, I have filled in the blank spaces,
learned you like a lesson as my own children grew.

This Is No Way to Live

My father, at ninety, says, "I'm worried. What's going to happen to me?" He is restless in his brown mechanical chair, sore and in pain from sitting all the time. His legs will not support him. They are paralyzed and lean together, the muscles withering so his feet appear large and swollen in his black, high-topped shoes. He tries to lift one foot off the floor, but cannot raise it for more than half an inch above the tan rug. "Ah," he says, "This is no way to live! I can't even write checks anymore. My hand shakes and I forget what I want to say." "Do you think," he asks, "that if I took three sleeping pills, I would just not wake up?" "Someday," he says, "I'm going to take some pills and go." I visit him each night. Stay with him for an hour. Sometimes, I just sit with him and cannot think of anything to say so I ask the same question three or four times. Sometimes, we talk politics, but lately he says, "It is too hard. I sit in this chair, then the aide lifts me out of the wheel chair. When it hurts too much to sit there, she moves me back here." "Don't worry, Dad," I say, "I worry." He says, "I worry about money. About where I will go if I get worse and I get worse every day. I worry, you know, even that there won't be room in heaven for me. Where can they fit all the people who died? I don't know," he says. "Mom'll be waiting for you. She'll find room for you," I say, "Eh, she was supposed to come back to get me," he says, "but she didn't. This is no life. Do you think if I took four sleeping pills it would be enough?"

No One Speaks His Language Anymore

I barely knew five words of English, when I went to school, spoke only the Southern Italian dialect we spoke at home. Now I have begun to forget the Italian words that chattered off my tongue when I was five and Italian was still the only language I really knew, but when I try to talk to my father, my Italian is as broken as his English, too many words I've forgotten or never knew. I keep asking my father to repeat the days of the week. I seem to be getting them confused. I wonder if my own brain cells are dying. My father understands me and I understand him, when I chatter in my pidgin Italian, and he asks me, "What am I here for, anyway, to go from this chair to the wheelchair and back again?" At ninety-one, all my father's friends are dead, my mother gone six years now, and all of us still grieving. How he longs for the days when he danced at the Società dinners and played *briscole* and *bocce* with his friends, the days when everyone spoke his language, and he was busy and happy, going to the Italian dinners and giving speeches, Italian all around him, wrapping him in its softness, beckoning to him with gestures he didn't need an interpreter to understand.

My Father Always Smelled of Old Spice

My father always smelled of Old Spice,
the skin of his face clear and unlined.
He used a bristle brush
and lather in a cup to shave,
a long-handled razor.
I used to watch him shave,
in his sleeveless undershirt,
his pants on, the suspenders
hanging down over his hips,
the straight razor making
swift smooth strokes down his cheeks.
He lifted his head back to reach under
his chin, then he'd slap on
Old Spice, the smell following
wherever he went.

My father always looked so clean,
his face magnolia white
against kinky black hair,
his big Italian nose,
a hook that made his face strong,
his flashing smile, the smile
of a handsome ladies man
though now the only ladies
who follow him are Gianni,
the Polish lady he pays to take care of him
since he can't walk anymore,
and Lillian and Dorothy, two of my brother's
patients, who visit my father
once every few weeks for an hour
though they are thirty years younger than he.
Sometimes they play cards
or just chat, my father's charm

and love of women evident
in the graciousness with which he welcomes them.

Even now, at ninety-one, my father's skin is still clear
and clean, but his mouth turns down
at the corners. He is disgruntled
and unhappy, wants to be done with it,
this life that for him has become
a burden not worth carrying.
His smile, even for me, when I walk into his house
each night, his smile has changed.
His eyes are hooded and he seems closed in
to his own private cell. "I'm tired," he says.
"It's too much for me," One night, we all go over
to see him, my daughter, her husband, and me,
and then my brother comes in with his son,
and my father for a few minutes becomes
his outgoing, gregarious self.
He tells us about his life, and we listen,
and as we are leaving, he says,
"Now I can sleep," and he is grinning
 his old grin, his face luminous.

This Morning

This morning, in the classroom with its neat and cheery bulletin board, I remember your voice on my telephone answering machine. You leave me a flip message, say you are at your friend's house so I can't call you back. You laugh and I hear your friend laughing, but I know that you are delivering a message not to call you, that you can't talk and I wonder where Paul is. Why isn't he with you? I worry that you are unhappy. Questions line up like Civil War soldiers in my head; then the phone rings again and it is Grandpa who is trying very hard to be independent since Grandma died and who's too proud to admit he is needy. "Well," he says, "I just called to see how you are." I say, "I just got home from work and it is 9 P.M. and I need to get ready for the festival." In clear, carefully enunciated English, he says, "It doesn't matter. I just called to see how you are." I can almost feel him standing up straight, his pride holding him away from me. All these connections, like the dotted lines in a child's story book, that hold us together, my need for Jennifer, my father's need for me.

In the Extravagant Kingdom of Words

In the extravagant kingdom of words
I am born again and again into delight,
the words carrying me out of myself
so that I become translucent as a white veil.
The sound of trucks moving fast distracts me,
and a bee buzzing and footsteps,
and hearing in my mind my son John's voice
on the phone, the argument we had over politics,
and I think why didn't I shut up?
I should have kept quiet
instead of talking about politics.
I should have changed the subject
when all I care about is this son of mine,
this son of mine who has moved away
with his wife and daughter
and they've been gone three weeks,
and now I fight with him.

I see him as a young boy,
remember sitting on his bed, holding his hand
and talking on the night before he goes off to college,
how he needed me then to be there.
I think of losing him,
how he's drifting away,
first to Washington and then in two years
to North Carolina, and taking his daughter,
that Caroline I have grown to love, with him,
and he, so distant, whom I held in my arms
and rocked the whole night through.

Opening the Door: 19th Street, Paterson

The crumbling cement steps led down to the dark cave of the cellar where the mouse traps waited in the corners and the big, iron coal furnace squatted next to the coal bin. My father used a shovel to scoop the coal out; it made a scraping sound, iron on cement, and the coal rattling. When he opened the little door of the furnace and threw in the coal, the flames rose up, and the heat poured out. In the back of the cellar was a room made out of scrap wood where my father made wine each summer, the cellar reeking of fermenting wine, his arms bulging when he carried in the heavy boxes of purple grapes. I told my brother there was a secret room in the cellar, like the secret rooms in the mansions in Nancy Drew novels, except our house was an old, imitation Victorian house cut up into apartments. In my mind, I could open up the little door behind the furnace, and step into a magic world far removed from the dank ordinary cellar. The life of 19th Street with its factory workers and drunks, the people next door who fought and screamed constantly. The world of my mother's life where she kept us confined to the front porch, but, through that door, everything I was not and wanted to be waited for me, and who knew, who knew to what dangerous, exciting places it would lead?

Learning Silence

By the time I was in first grade, I knew enough
to be frightened, to keep my hands folded
on my desk and try to be quiet "as a mouse."
I am nervous most of the time,
feel sick to my stomach.
I am afraid to raise my hand, afraid
to ask for the bathroom pass, afraid
of the bigger children, but, most of all,
afraid of Miss Barton who does not like me.

We read the *Dick and Jane* books. The world of these books,
painted in bright primary colors, seems so free and perfect.
When I open the pages, I feel I can walk through them,
like Alice stepping through the looking glass,
into that clean world,
those children with their wide open faces,
their blonde curls, their cute, skipping legs,
their black and white dog with its perky tail,
their big, white house with its huge lawn of manicured grass.
In those books, I can forget Miss Barton and her icy
eyes and the grimy, shopworn classrooms of PS 18,
with their scarred wooden desks,
their dark green blackout shades,
reminders of the war that has just ended.
In that house, where even the doghouse is perfect,
there would be no reason to be afraid.

I try to be good. I try to be quiet.
I hope Miss Barton will not curl her lip
when she looks at me.
I would gladly turn into Jane
if some magic could transform me,
make me blonde and cute, instead of sad
and serious and scared, with my sausage curls
my huge, terrified eyes,
my long nose, my dark, olive-toned skin,
the harsh cheap cotton of my clothes.

The Surprise Party

When I was eleven, Judy gave a surprise party for me. I think she felt guilty because when we were really little girls, we had been best friends, but then she grew beautiful and sophisticated and I stayed a little girl much longer than she did. Judy became friends with other girls like her, girls who were beautiful and sure of themselves and who knew how to talk to boys and to flirt and who had mothers who bought fashionable and expensive clothes for them. One Sunday, Judy invited me to her house. I walked there from 19th Street. For as long as I could remember I had lived on 17th Street, in the two family house across the street from Judy's house, but when I was eleven, my mother and father bought a two family house two blocks away on 19th Street and we moved there. I missed 17th Street, felt cut off from my old friends, the boys and girls who caught fireflies in the summer dusk and roller skated on the slate sidewalk in front of the shoemaker's shop on Third Avenue, the shoemaker, who would be shot thirty years later, still sitting in his dirty little shop that smelled of shoe leather and polish, an odor both sweet and tart.

That Sunday, the Sunday of my surprise party, I ran up the back steps of Judy's house, and she ran down to meet me and said, "Let's go downstairs; we can play in the back," meaning the back room of the bar that her grandfather and father and uncles rented out for showers and birthday parties, and where we often played on rainy days, sliding on the polished wood floors, the muffled sounds of the bar to hold us in.

Judy ran into the back room first and I followed. She switched on the lights, and up jumped Camille and Andrea and Diane and Dorothy and all the other girls from the sixth grade, yelling, "Surprise! Surprise!" and I was surprised that they planned the party for me and happy and embarrassed at being the center of attention. There were balloons, streamers, sodas, and cake. We played pin the tail on the donkey and sang songs and whispered and giggled and I felt included again, though they seemed to know secrets I had not yet learned about boys and how to dress, and they didn't look foreign the way my mirror told me I did, and I could not know then, standing, surrounded by girls I hoped were my friends, and by Judy who had planned the party for me, what would happen to them later or to me, but it is Judy who remains clearest in my memory, Judy who met her boyfriend on the bus when she was going to Benedictine Academy. Judy whose boyfriend gave her a black eye and she told her father she had walked into a door. Judy, blonde, blue-eyed and graceful, whose boyfriend broke her arm and she told everyone they had a car accident. Judy who ran away and married her boyfriend when she turned sixteen, and her father who adored her was so distressed his hair turned white overnight. Judy, who ten years later, when I met her at St. George's festival, walking with her husband and five children, was so fat she could hardly move. I was with my husband and two children; I was 110 pounds and considered myself to be fat. We stopped to talk. I told her Dennis was finishing his doctorate and we'd be moving to Kansas City where he'd teach at the university. She said her husband was a pipe fitter in a factory.

Years later, she called me to say that she'd stayed with her husband for ten years. The last time he put her in the hospital she decided not to go back. "I loved him," she said, "that's why I stayed so long. He was exciting." She tells me she remarried. "My husband is good to me," she says. After a few minutes, we don't know what to say to each other. "You did so well," she says, and I think of how intelligent she was, how quick to pick up ideas, how bubbly and beautiful. "I've settled down now," she says, her voice flat, all trace of that golden girl gone and she, whose life should have opened for her, unrolled like a bridal carpet, instead closed in on her, while mine sprang open and let me go free.

Training Bra

When I was eleven, I wore white cotton undershirts,
serviceable and plain. All winter
I wore one under my school blouse; in summer,
I wore one as my only garment,
tucked into my shorts with elastic around my waist.
One day, I came running in from playing tag on 19th Street,
and my mother said, "You can't wear that shirt outside
    anymore."
The next day she took me to Jacobs Department Store
to buy me a training bra. I was proud of it,
a symbol that I was growing up.

"I got her a training bra," my mother whispered to my aunt,
and asked me to lift my shirt to show it off. They both smiled
and exchanged a look I could not read, half proud, half
    exultant.
"You're a woman now," my aunt said, and when she said it, I
    knew
some petty meanness in her was glad that I was caught too
as she had been caught in the life of a woman, the training bra
the beginning of constrictions, all the snaps and hooks
designed to train us to accept the boundaries
of the women we would become.

Zia Concetta and Her Whalebone Corset

Zia Concetta always wore a flesh-colored whalebone corset, the white bone stays circling her heavy body and the laces pulled tight so there was no jiggling but only a fullness, hard and contained. That corset held in all Zia's life, her four husbands, all of them dead, except the last one, handsome and silent, a slender, elegant man who hid from her in the garden or in the wooden shed at the end of the yard where he carved elaborate bird houses and wind pointers and she raged at him, calling his name from the second story stoop into the summer dusk.

Wearing starched housedresses over her corset, she walked each day to Ferraro's Coat Factory where she sewed coats by hand and laughed her deep belly laugh with my mother and the other women. Some evenings, she cooked spaghetti dinners with the Ladies Auxiliary of the Società and, after the dishes were washed, she danced the tarantella, her feet stamping the floor in her high heeled shoes, her body twirling, her upper lip beaded with sweat gleaming in her bleached mustache. I can still see her little white handkerchief, a triangle that she tucked up her sleeve and used to pat away the sweat. She seemed so alive, with her shining eyes and her copper hair and her jokes and funny stories, but there was always a mystery at the center of her life, the sound of wild sobbing my mother said she heard coming through the floor.

We lived on the first floor and she and my uncle on the second. Each night my mother would hear Zìa crying and pleading, until finally there was silence and the house slept, and though they were friends, she and my mother, in the morning Zia would come downstairs in her starched dress and she'd be smiling and laughing. She never spoke of what happened each night. Perhaps that corset was meant not so much to contain excess flesh but to hold in all the secrets, the things a woman couldn't say for fear her life would fall apart so she laughed that laugh in my kitchen when my mother made me lift my shirt to show her my training bra, and she said, "Oh, now you're a woman," and I knew she was exulting that I, too, would learn the lessons of tears shed in darkness, of lies hidden behind closed doors, all the things I'd have to learn to hold in.

First Dance at the CYO

At twelve I went to the CYO dance in the basement of Blessed Sacrament Church on 16th Street in Paterson, NJ. The jukebox was playing a romantic song by Johnny Mathis. I can't remember the song, only that it filled me with longing, sad and sweet and glorious. Janet, who moved into Paterson when I was in seventh grade just at the moment when all the girls who had been my friends discovered boys and sophistication I so obviously didn't have became my best friend. She got me by default and I got her the same way.

She knew a lot more about boys than I did and told me about it though I still didn't understand much. At this CYO dance, the eighth grade girls talked in small cliques with each other and the high school kids stood around on the other side of the hall, fooling around and talking to the young priest who chaperoned us. This was when girls still danced together, the jitterbug and other fast dances, and when Johnny Mathis voice filled the hall, Janet and I moved out on the floor and danced together, a slower version of a dance I can't remember though it was a forerunner to rock and roll. What I do remember is dancing with her and listening to Johnny Mathis syrupy voice imagining that I was dancing, not with plain-faced Janet, thin and wiry, a tough freckled street kid who already had a boyfriend named Joe and hinted that they'd done it, making jokes about Vaseline that I didnt understand. I looked over, saw John R, the huge football player from the high school team pointing to us, laughing, and I realized that he'd seen my dreamy face and he was making jokes about us. The iridescent moment broke for me. And I knew how stupid I looked to him, how vulnerable in my dreamy, twelve-year old heart.

First Trip to the Jersey Shore:
Long Branch, NJ

Every year when the silk mills closed in July, and everyone we knew went to the Jersey shore, we stayed home. We didn't own a car and even I knew we were poor, but when I was thirteen, suddenly, my mother agreed to go to the shore for a week with my aunt and my grown cousins. My cousin Joey drove. I sat in the back seat and tried not to be sick. Fifteen minutes from home, Joey had to stop the car so I could throw up at the side of the road. The Parkway hadn't been built yet. It took hours to get to the huge, white Victorian boarding house, with its graceful, wrap-around porch, its turrets and peaked towers and widow's walk. We slept in one room, my aunt and her family in another. Between the rooms, a shared bath with a claw-footed tub. My mother left Italy when she was twenty-three. Before that she never left San Mauro, the little town in Campania where she was born. When she married my father, he brought her to an Italian neighborhood in Paterson; she refused to leave it, felt safe only in her own house and was so terrified of the ocean that every time we went near the water, she screamed, "Watch out! You'll drown." Through the open windows of the boarding house, we could smell the salt of the sea, tangy and sweet. We shared one kitchen with all the other families. The silver was kept in glasses on the counter; the napkins in a circular holder. Most evenings we walked on the quiet, empty boardwalk at Long Branch and watched the sea. One night, Joey drove us to Seaside Heights to that teeming boardwalk with its neon lights and loud, jostling crowds. We were given a dollar apiece to spend on the games of chance or the ferris wheel. We wandered into the souvenir shops to look; we didn't buy anything. I saw a cedar keepsake box stamped Long Branch, New Jersey. I wanted it, but I only asked one time. My mother said, "No." The night before we were to leave Long Branch, my mother pushed the cedar box into my hands, said,

"Here. This is for you," and turned away. I loved that box, kept it for years. The smooth, sweet, aroma of cedar wood rose to meet me each time I opened it, made me remember the shore and the tangy aroma of salt air and my mother who turned away when she gave me that cedar box, though not before I saw her smile.

Glittering As We Fall

The glittering net skirt I got from my cousin
Carmela for my thirteenth birthday. Even the box
was beautiful, glossy cherry red and tied
with a slender gold cord and Lord & Taylor
stamped in gold letters, curved and graceful,
in the center. Inside the sturdy box,
not at all like the boxes my mother got
from The Mart or Woolworth's, the thick layers
of tissue paper, and then the long red net skirt
that shimmered every time I moved. Carmela said,
"Now you can have a party."
I felt lifted into the more sophisticated realm
of beauty. So I planned a party and invited my friends
from high school. My mother made a cake and cookies
and pitchers of Kool Aid. On the night of the party,
I picked up the telephone to call my friend Pat and,
by some quirk or tangle of lines,
my call went directly to her line. I heard
her speaking to the boy she was dating.
"I don't want to go to her dumb party,"
she said. "It will be a party for little kids.
Gosh, her mother will be there!" "Say you're sick
and can't go. Meet me instead," he said.
I hung up the phone. A few minutes later,
the phone rang. Pat told me she couldn't
come to the party. She was sick, she said.
Three or four others called to say they weren't coming.
My best friend Lois and her boyfriend Bill called last.
I cannot remember what excuse they used.
My family pretended that nothing happened.

We ate the cake and cookies, drank Kool Aid,
and played Monopoly all evening. It was only
as I was getting ready for bed that I buried my face
in my cats fur and cried till I fell asleep.

You Were Always Escaping

You were always escaping.
We'd hear the sound of the brown door
slamming, the rattle of glass panes,
and you would vanish.

I see us standing in the 17th Street kitchen,
Mamma with her arm around us
and her bruised eyes.
Her voice quivering, she'd say,
"Can't you stay home tonight?"
staring at the empty doorway,
then she'd sigh, lift her shoulders,
and begin some project with us.

She'd give us cookie cutters
shaped like stars and bells,
and we'd cut out sugar cookies,
even Alex who was only three.

We'd dye sugar red with food coloring
and sprinkle it on top. The kitchen
would fill with the sweet aroma
of our baking, and we were content.

Other times, we'd make chocolate pudding
or listen to Stella Dallas on the radio.
Sometimes, she'd lift Alessandro into her lap,
and Laura and I would perch on the arms
of the old padded rocker, and she'd tell us stories
about San Mauro, the town where she grew up.
Through the evening hours, she would distract herself
as well as us, but once we were in our beds,

her hunger for your presence
would return and smear the contented landscape.

During the day, you swept the halls
of Central High School, mopped the floors,
picked up the refuse in the Boys and Girls bathrooms.
At lunch time, you sat in on algebra
and history classes but you were subservient,
your head bent, humble. Though you were louder,
Mamma ruled the house. But at the Società
your friends looked up to you, and you were proud
of your speeches at political dinners,
your awards, and standing ovations.

"You always choose your friends first," Mamma hissed,
her voice rising with anger, and you would struggle
from her grasp, rushing to the next meeting,
the evenings playing *bocce* at the Società
the spaghetti dinners, the women
of the Ladies Auxillary
who flirted with you
while Mamma stayed home.

Mamma peered out of the edge
of the green blackout shades,
waited for your footsteps
on the wooden porch.

Even when you stayed home one evening,
you were restless pacing the floor
as though the kitchen were a cage
and we the bars that tried to hold you
but that always failed.

Marilyn Monroe and My Sister

When I was a girl, we all wanted to look like Marilyn Monroe, with her hourglass figure, her pouty mouth, her exquisite face, her huge eyes. At thirteen, my sister looked like Marilyn. She even had the same slender legs, the sexy breasts, tiny waist, the clear exquisite skin, the full sensuous lips. When my sister graduated from PS 18, she wore a black eyelet dress that she made herself. All the girls had to make their own dresses. If her hair had been blonde rather than brown, she could have been Marilyn. My sister won a baby beauty contest when she was two, her skin and eyes and mouth, perfect even then. In our pictures when we were young, I look almost electric with life, my hair a mass of black ringlets, my eyes bright. My sister looks beautiful. I remember Marilyn Monroe with her breathy voice, her way of looking at men, that photograph of her that we all still see, Marilyn standing over the subway grate, her knees bent, her skirt revealing her legs, and every time I looked at her I knew I could never look at a man the way she did, talk to him in that sexy voice, my body too slender, my walk too matter of fact, my shyness leaving my face and body stiff. Oh, I wanted to walk like her, my hips swinging, but I looked from Marilyn to my sister as we sat in the Fabian theatre, and I saw that there was a sexy musk about them. I knew they were born knowing a secret I would never know.

My Father's First Car

My father's first car was a ten-year old Chevy, dark blue with gray upholstery. He had it repainted from rusty black to dark blue at Car Coat Body Painters:

WE PAINT YOUR CAR
SO IT LOOKS BRAND NEW.

The car had bumps and ridges where the paint bubbled. The upholstery was torn, but my mother made slipcovers from left-over remnants of cloth, a pattern of odd-looking diamonds, orange and gray. The interior of the car, like our house, was spot-less. I was thirteen when my father bought the car second hand. The next week, it broke down and he had to have it repaired. It had more than 100,000 miles on it, and he couldn't drive when he bought it. One of his friends took him out on the road to teach him. The car was a shift. My father's left leg was partially para-lyzed. It dragged when he walked. He wore heavy black ortho-pedic shoes that had black soles and laced up the front. They were like the boots that young people wear today and came up over his ankle. They helped him to walk, but still one leg dragged. The paralysis in his leg was a problem in using a car with manu-al transmission. Despite the fact that he didn't speak English, he managed to pass the driver's test after two tries. The first time he couldn't understand the English that the driving test officer spoke so he turned in the wrong direction and failed. The next time he passed. The officer was kinder. He spoke slowly. My father rejoiced that he passed the test. And we all went off with him for a drive around Riverside.

My father's first car changed our lives. The world opened up a little for us, though we still walked everywhere, my father reserved the car for driving to work and the market and for picking us up from school when he could. My father's first car huffed and puffed, and often spewed black smoke from the exhaust, though my father took it to be repaired repeatedly. My mother made a pillow for my father, stuffed it with cut up strips of cotton from clothes too worn out to wear. Without the cushion my father was too short to see over the top of the dashboard. To help him out so that he could reach the pedals, she wrapped them in cotton cloth so they'd be easier for him to reach.

We three kids would sit in the back seat, my mother sat in the front, her head like a small knob barely reaching the top of the seat. No one was allowed to talk except my mother who would warn my father when she thought another car was going to hit us or that he hadn't seen a light, though she'd never driven a car in her life and was always terrified in one, one hand hanging on to the door handle, her pocketbook over the other arm, her legs rigid and her feet pushing down on the floor. Because his leg was weak, my father drove in fits and starts, the car lurching forward and hitching back and we were quiet in the backseat, happy to be going somewhere, even to the market or to visit our aunt who lived too many blocks away to walk. My father's first car was our chariot. It opened a door for us that once it was opened would never be closed again. We didn't know how we looked to others, my father, feeling important behind the wheel, able to offer rides now to other friends who didn't have a car, and when he drove, he didn't smile. He concentrated all his attention on driving. As soon as he stopped and put the car in park and raised the handbrake into place, he would grin and sigh, happy to have arrived. When he got out, he always patted the fender. How much walking that car saved him, dragging that leg that only moved because he forced it to.

The Moment I Knew My Life Had Changed

It was not until later
that I knew, recognized the moment
for what it was, my life before it,
a gray landscape, shapeless and misty;
my life after, flowering full and leafy
as the cherry trees that only today
have torn into bloom.

Imagine: my cousin at nineteen, tall,
slender. She worked in New York City.
For my thirteenth birthday she took me
to New York. We ate at the Russian Tea Room
where I was uncertain about which fork to use,
intimidated by the women in their hats and furs,
by the waiters who watched me
as I struggled with the huge hunk of bread
in the center of the onion soup in its steep bowl.
When we were ready to leave, I tried to give the tip
back to my cousin. I thought she had forgotten it.
She said, "No, its for the waiter!"

On 57th Street a man in a camel coat bumped into me,
rushed on by. My cousin said, "That was Eddie Fisher,"
but I said, "Hes too short. It can't be."
I felt let down that Eddie Fisher,
the star I was in love with that year, was so rude
he never even said, "Excuse me." Then we went into the theater
sat in the front row. The stage sprang into colored light,
and the glittery costumes, the singing, the magical story,
drew me in, made me feel in that moment,
what I would learn again and again,
the miraculous language, the music of it.
My life, turning away from the constricted world

of the 19th Street tenement, formed a line
almost perpendicular to that old life,
I moved toward it, breathed in this new air,
racing toward a world filled with poems and
music and books that freed me from everything
that could have chained me to the ground.

When We Were Girls

When we were girls, we talked about songs and movies,
what Amelia said to Jean, who was dating Joe,
what skirt we saw and why we bought it or didn't.
We talked together walking in twos or threes
down Main, past Meyer Brothers to Berman's
where we looked at the cashmere sweaters,
fingering their soft luxury but never buying.

We hung around as long as we could
or until we saw one of the other girls walk in,
one of the girls who really could afford to buy
one of those coveted sweaters in their soft pastels,
those sweaters that spelled life in a big Dutch colonial
in the Eastside section with parents who owned
the factories where our parents worked.

We pretended to be happy and casual
as we scuttled out into the street
heading for the Mart with its tacky clothes
and its saleswomen who rushed up to ask,
"May I help you?" and who wore too much make-up
and told us we looked good in that dress
even when we didn't.

When we were girls, I talked my mother into buying
me a pale pink angora sweater for my birthday.
It wasn't one of those cashmere ones,
but as close as I was likely to get.
When I put it on and looked at myself
in the dresser mirror, I knew that pale pink
which would have looked wonderful on a blonde
drained my sallow skin of all light.
When we were girls, even after I saw

the sweater was all wrong for me,
we still went into Berman's every chance we got,
still believed that the right sweater
would transform us.

My Funny Valentine

"My Funny Valentine" plays on the juke box
in the student lounge at Seton Hall University.
Sinatra's voice fills me with longing
to be someone's funny valentine, to imagine
that Andy will ask me out on a real date
instead of to a dance, that he will do more than lean
his thin body against the limestone facade of the college
    building,
and hold a cigarette in his long, nervous fingers
while he talks to me about classes or his after school job.

We work together editing the college paper
in the little office the school allows us to use.
Near him in that cramped space, I learn
his narrow face,
his thatch of black hair,
his blade of a nose,
the quirky energetic way he moves.

My funny valentine or as close as I come
that freshman year when Andy takes me
to the Christmas dance and kisses me
in the back of Bill Klingdorfer's car,
borrowed from his father, the feel of the Buick's
rough tweed upholstery on my bare arms,
the crackle of my satin party dress,
Andy's thin lips pressed on my mouth.

So safe to love, my funny valentine,
who could kiss me with his lips closed in the back seat
of Bill's Buick and not kindle one spark in me,
and who gives me someone to moon over
while Sinatra's voice fills me with molten heat.

Work

Every morning, my father drove me to Manhattan Shirt Factory on River Street where I worked in the summer after freshman year. My job was to take down the number on the inside of the collars of returned shirts and clip tags to them and then set them into bins according to the reason for their return. The shirts were often dirty, sweat stained and smelly, as though someone had worn them for days before returning them. The supervisor walked up and down behind the sorters in the small room lit by bare light bulbs hanging from cords attached to the exposed beams. No one spoke and dust was thick in the rancid air. When the wind was blowing in the right direction, the smell of the polluted Passaic River filled the room. The windows, covered by a metal grill, were grimy and caked with greasy dirt. Very little light entered. A loud buzzer signaled the start of our half hour lunch. We rushed outside to sit on the front steps or stand, leaning against the factory wall, and eat our lunch. No one talked to me. The others joked around with one another and occasionally one would say, "Watch out, you're embarrassing the college kid," but mostly they ignored me. At the sound of another buzzer, we retreated into the darkness of the mill and emerged again only at four when the work-day was over. In between, we sorted dirty shirts. I hated to pick them up and I kept trying to hold my breath so I wouldn't have to smell them. In a few weeks, the boss came in and told me he wanted me to work in the other plant packing new skirts into boxes. The factory was a twin of the first, except it was on the top of a hill. Finished skirts came toward me on a conveyer belt like the kind in dry cleaning stores. I had to lift each skirt off the rack and pack it neatly in its special carton. This involved standing up all day and by four o'clock I was ready to collapse, my legs and arms aching. Sometimes, a few minutes before the ending buzzer was to go off, the harsh voice of the supervisor would shout "overtime." The regular workers seemed to me to be gray and wizened – was it the dust or the noise that did it, or never being outside? Anyway when the supervisor called for overtime, the other workers were happy for the extra hours, the time and a half pay, but I thought I'd scream if I had to stay an extra hour. My father came to pick me up, and I complained about the place and how happy I'd be to leave it, and it never occurred to me that he and my mother had to work in a factory every day for more than forty-five years. I never heard either one of them complain, or mention the shouting supervisors, their rudeness, the lack of light, the incredible noise, the dust, the mindless repetition of the work or how often they must have felt like screaming but didn't because they couldn't afford the luxury. They thought about us and what they had to do, and kept their heads bent, their faces hidden, while they worked.

My First Car

My first car was a blue VW bug with a sunroof. I bought it used from a used car lot on Market Street and it should have been a rip-off but it wasn't. It was bright blue, and when I bought it I didn't know how to drive. I'd always taken the bus everywhere. My brother-in-law took me out to teach me how to drive it. I had one lesson before I drove it, bucking and kicking, to my first job after college. The office was in Elizabeth, and in order to reach it from Hawthorne, I had to drive down the Garden State Parkway, but my brother-in-law never got around to teaching me how to downshift so every time I had to change gears, I had to put the car into neutral, stop the car, and start over from first gear. I drove in the slow lane, that VW so shiny and perfect, the radio playing, the sun on my hair, the rides we took in it all over Bergen County, Barbara and Diane, Sandy and Mary, all of us squashed into that blue bug, all of us laughing and singing "One hundred bottles of beer on the wall" as loud as we could, stopping for pizza at Stasney's, and on the way home, late at night, the stars still visible in the Hawthorne sky, we sang along with Sinatra or Johnny Mathis, our longing thick as honey in the small world of the car. Looking back at us, myself and those young women who were my friends, I see us bathed in moonlight, our faces untouched by everything we had yet to learn, the future rushing toward us in the moonlit car, and we blissfully singing love songs and pretending to be happy.

The Family Car

We sold our blue VW bug
and bought a tan family sedan,
to go with our new lives as grown-ups,
married and with a two-year old
and a baby. We needed more room
for lugging a car bed and stroller,
an infant seat and diaper bag.

During the week, you spent your days
in a library carrel writing your dissertation.
I spent mine walking two children
through grocery stores and shopping centers.
I was lonely, though I loved the children,
the dimples on their elbows, their delighted laughs,
the quiet contained play of our two-year old,
the damp, milky sleep of the baby.

I escaped walking among other women
wheeling small children, walking
aimless and near tears down tiled aisles
where there was nothing I wanted
or could ever use.

We moved to Kansas City in that Plymouth
when you got your doctorate. You taught
at the university and we bought a house
near the campus so you could ride your bike
to classes while I used the car. That year
I made friends with a violinist
who had six children, including one adopted
from Korea. Her husband, an English professor,
studied Buddhist philosophy.

They lived in a big old house.
They slept on mattresses on the floor.
She practiced her violin for four hours a day.
The children were not allowed to disturb her.
She had a room at the back of the house
that was full of laundry drying on racks.
The children picked their clothes off the racks
each morning. They never washed the dishes
until there were no dishes left. "It's a waste
of time," she said. Chaos and disorder everywhere.

When her parents came to visit, they stayed
for two days in a motel; then they went back
to California. All the things I had been taught
were sacred – a clean house, clothes, neat and
ironed, the beds made first thing in the morning –
didn't matter at all to Anne, and I was horrified
and envied her that freedom that let her do
what she wanted without all those voices telling her
what was right and what was wrong, the voices
I carried with me wherever I went that sounded
suspiciously like my mother's voice.

Anne and David owned an old VW camper.
They read a lot when they went camping,
the children allowed to run wild and alone.
She worried about things like not putting water
in the wooden salad bowl, but not whether her children
would fall in the lake and drown.

Though we were twenty-eight years old, Dennis and I
were protected innocents, driving
a car that could have belonged to Dennis parents
and, suddenly, this glimpse into freedom made us afraid
that we were turning into his parents, so we traveled
every chance we got all over Colorado, Kansas, New Mexico,

trying to shed our tight and frightened skin,
trying to crack open our world
held fast by too many rules.

Family Vacations

When the children were little,
we bought a used VW camper,
gray with red upholstery
and a fold-down table.

We drove from Kansas City
through Kansas to Colorado
and across New Mexico
with its roadside stone markers
for its highway dead.

Once we got almost as far as Arizona.
We camped in a national park
next to an Indian reservation.

Every day an Indian family drove
their rusty pick-up into the park
and filled eight rusty barrels
with water. They didn't look
anything like movie Indians.

The mother of the family was squat
and barefoot. Two girls, maybe
eight and ten years old,
sat near the mother in the bed
of the truck. Two teenage boys rode
in the cab with a younger boy.

The mother's face, high cheekboned
and stoic, was impassive. She pretended
to be blind, doing what she had to do.
Seeing her, I remember walking with my mother
down Main Street. I spoke to her in Italian,

people stared, and I heard someone hiss,
"Why don't they speak English?"
This woman could be my mother,
wearing that same impassioned dignity,
their pride too great to accept pity.
I tried not to let her see. I watched instead

as the boys arms, bulging with new muscles,
lifted the heavy barrels onto the truck.
The little girls sat, barefoot
and solemn, watching.
They lived on the reservation because they had to
while we roughed it for a few days
in our camper with its fold-down bed
and the small beds we made for our small children.

The day was hot and still; then a dust storm
swept our campsite. The red sand burned
and stung. And the one
stunted tree bent and twisted in the wind.
We rushed for the camper, herding the children
and ourselves inside and huddled there,
helpless against such fury,
the sand hitting the windows like hail
and the wind swaying the camper
while the children cried.

Suddenly, I'd had enough of adventure,
wanted only to take our children out
of those huge empty spaces,
the enormous bowl of the thunderous sky,
and back to the safety of our old house,
with its thick plaster walls and back stair
and big sunny windows
and sidewalks and hedges,
the other Oak Street houses protecting us

from all that unflinching space that told us
how small we were,
how little we could do.

Secrets

In my family, we never told our secrets, our lives
hidden like the undersides of leaves.
Even today, though I talk to my sister a lot,
though she tells me little facts about her life,
mostly I remain private and hidden and afraid.
I, who can write out every secret in a poem,
never tell anyone anything.

In our family, our pride too great to admit how vulnerable we
   are,
we follow my mother's example.
She demanded that we keep our spines straight,
our feet on the floor, but I remember arguments so loud,
our neighbors would stare at us for days.
My mother always pretended nothing happened.

In our house, I was always afraid
my mother wouldn't approve of me.
So many lies I told to cover up
the things my mother's rules would not allow,
how I wanted to crack out of that cast of rules,
the things a person could and could not do,

So how could I tell the truth about the night
when I slept over at Anne's house?
We went to New York City to see a play
and we missed the last train.
We had to spend the night
in the train station in Hoboken.
The bums who slept there kept asking,
"What are nice girls like you doing here?"
In the morning, after being afraid
to sleep all night, men reeking of alcohol

peering into our faces, we walked at dawn
to the Catholic Church, went to the six o'clock mass,
and then caught the first train to Ridgewood

where Anne's parents were waiting for us,
both of them furious in a stiff, middle-class way,
saying, "Why didn't you call?"
and Anne saying, "I thought you'd be asleep."
"We were up all night," her mother hissed at her,

I wanted to crawl under their dining room table,
only glad that this icy anger was directed at Anne
and not at me, glad that my mother didn't know.

Though I'd come to my mother's house sometimes
when I was a grown woman myself
and sit in her kitchen, sobbing,
unable to stop or explain.
She held me, asking, "What is it?
What is it? Cry. Cry. It will be good
for you. What is it?" and I,
unable to say.

The Perfect Mother

Ma, now that you are five years dead, now that I have turned you into the perfect mother, the larger-than-life mother, have I forgiven you for saying, "If I don't tell you who will?" and for telling me everything that is wrong with me as soon as I walk in the door, "You should wear some make-up," you'd say. "That skirt makes you look fat. You and those books, forget those books! Why don't you stay home?" I asked you not to tell me even for my own good, and you did try, but of course you couldn't help yourself. Still the crow who sits on my shoulder, the crow who has your voice whispers in my ear everything that is wrong with me.

And have I forgiven you, Ma, who carried us all on your back; Ma, who loved us singlemindedly and never said it. Ma, who did not crack under ten-hour days sewing in sleeves by hand in the dusty coat factories of Paterson; Ma who scrubbed and cleaned our clothes on a tin washboard, and who washed my hair so completely I thought my scalp would come off; Ma, who ironed and starched our dresses; Ma, who saved and scrimped, and never bought anything for yourself; Ma, who baked bread and gave it to us hot out of the oven, butter from the Lakeview Dairy crock melting over it; Ma, who rose at five each morning to cook dinner and bake bread, and left at eight for the coat factory, and came home and worked in the house until you went to bed; Ma, who fell on a roller skate, walked to the coat factory and back at noon to make our lunches and walked back again and finished out the afternoon and collapsed with ten broken bones in your foot and you didn't cry.

Ma, how can I be angry with you for something you couldn't help? How can I not forgive you, when you taught me so much about how to take the next step even when you think you can't move one inch more? Healer, seer, powerhouse that you were, woman who taught me how to laugh, if I cannot forgive this one flaw what will my children find in me that will still anger them even years after my eye becomes opaque as milk glass, and turns inward as yours did in that hospital cubicle where I held your hand while you died? How I miss coming to you, just to be near you, that strength that was more comforting than any wine, you in your kitchen, pouring me an espresso and cutting up a peach for me, Ma, forgive this scarf of anger that floats to the surface when I least expect, forgive it because you know I wish I could be with you again in your basement kitchen, one more time, you working and criticizing and laughing, you warm as the spring sun in my face.

The Two-Dollar Housedress

I imagine my mother wearing a two-dollar housedress,
crisp with starch. She owned two or three of them.
She washed them on the scrubboard in the kitchen sink
and hung them out to dry in the sun. Then she poured
liquid starch into a basin, sprinkled it
on the dress, heated the iron on the coal stove,
and ironed the dresses to crispness.

Sometimes I'd go to Meyer Brothers and look
at the housedresses there. I knew my mother's dresses
were much cheaper looking, the flowers on them
not as pretty, the material so coarse
it scratched my skin. I think of the years
of those inexpensive dresses, and of the satin dress,

red satin, rich and creamy, my mother bought for me
to wear to the freshman Christmas dance. The red dress
brightened my sallow face.
The cut of the dress,
the darts on the bodice
the nipped in waist setoff my small high breasts,
my size twenty-three waist,
the subtle roundness of slender hips.
I loved the way it moved around me when I walked,
and how beautiful I felt in it, and now,

with my mother five years dead, I realize
I never thanked her
for the stiff housedresses she wore for years,
for the twenty-five dollar dress for me she couldn't afford
but bought anyway, for teaching me how to look
at my children as she looked at me, her eyes saying,

"Oh, you are beautiful in the dress," and, for that one moment when I believed her.

In the Pages of a Photo Album

In an imaginary album, I see pictures of you
as a baby. I am holding you, my body
almost curled around you,
I am sitting
in Grandma's flowered wing chair
in the River Edge house.
In another picture,
though you are only two years old,
you are tugging at my hands, already trying
to pull away. In each photo, you grow

older, the hours, days, months between
cast into shadow – you in grammar school
in the blue St. Anthony's uniform,
your shirt pulled out of your pants,
and you on a boy scout camping trip,
Joey and Bobby and Chris and Richie,
all of you caught in motion; you
with Grandpa at your high school graduation,
you at the prom, at college graduation,
law school, the years ripping off
some incredible roll of days
until today, I try to imagine

you in Washington, but unlike the pictures
of your childhood, the image is blurred,
as though I were looking at it
through a scratched lens. When we speak,
I struggle as if I were speaking to a person
I barely know, the conversation so heavy
it is a sack of stone and, all the time,
even when the tears are rolling madly down,
my face, even when we disagree on everything

and every word I say detonates like a bomb,
my love for you ignites, persistent
and unreasonable as tulips that burst into flame
each spring out of frozen ground.

If I Had the Courage, I'd Ask My Children What They Remember About Me When They Were Growing Up

Memory opens like a hand inside me, and all the secrets I cannot bear to know spill out. Remember: the children in grammar school – their untucked shirts, their ill-cut unkempt hair, John with his crooked grin and his wide teeth, and Jennifer at seven, her curls vanished, her hair chopped off by Laura in an awkward pageboy. Remember: the laundry basket spilling clothes in rumpled profusion, the mad search for lost shoes in the morning, the cold cereal, the books everywhere, tinker toys and dust. Not that I did not love them, not that I did not do what I could, inept maker of braids, slovenly housewife, descended from a long line of women brilliant at housekeeping, a glitch in the genetic chain.

How my mother complained that I let them walk barefoot in summer, let them leap on the couch, slide down the banister, play wild games in the living room. How I rolled on the floor with them, laughed at our private jokes, made funny faces for them. "Mom, come on, Mom," and I went, driving them to boy scouts and overnight campouts, to parties and friends' houses, driving them to private schools outside the county, track meets and theater groups and gymnastics. How I wanted them to live up to the promise of their incredible beauty, the clear, clean lines of their faces, the wide violet lakes of their eyes.

How did I fail them who loved them so much? How many other ways that I cannot even imagine? My son, whom I cannot talk to, my son, who seems so distant from me, your daughter plasters herself against your chest, clings to your neck, pushes herself so close to your body there is no room for air. Her face is luminous and content. You call me more often now, though we still struggle to form a language we both understand. What do you say to me now that you have a child of your own?

Yesterday

Yesterday, I saw a young woman walking
with a small boy, perhaps two or three
years old; she is holding his hand.
They are happy. Remembering them,
I think of you as a little boy,
your hand in mine.

I cannot see all the years ahead, swollen
and waiting to erupt toward me;
instead I am sure you are mine
forever, my love for you so great
I cannot imagine a time
when you will move away from me,
sleek as a fish and as slippery,

so that now, when you call me
from Washington, my voice cracks
under the weight of all I want to say
and cannot, and when I try,
when I push past your image of yourself
as a grown man and a father
and of myself as your mother
still holding that small boys hand,
what I say is all wrong.

When I replace the receiver, I think
of my mother, see her clearly
as if she were in the room with me,
and wish I could call her back
from the dead, could tell her,

twenty years late, how each word
aimed like a dart is repaid in kind,
just as she said.

Love Poem to My Husband
of Thirty-One Years

I watch you walk up our front path,
the entire right side of your body
stiff and unbending, your leg
dragging on the ground,
your arm not moving.
Six different times you ask me
the date of our daughter's wedding,
seem surprised each time,
forget who called, though you can name
obscure desert animals,
and every detail of events
that took place in 3 B.C.
You complain now of pain
in your muscles, of swimming at the Y
where a seventy-six year old man tells you
you swim too slowly.
I imagine a world in which
you cannot move.

Most days, I force myself to look
only into the past;
remember you, singing
and playing your guitar: "Black,
black is the color of my true loves hair,"
you sang, and each time you came into a room
how my love for you caught in my throat,
how handsome you were, how strong
and muscular, how the sun
lit your blond hair.

Now I pretend not to notice
the trouble you have buttoning
your shirt, and, yes, I am terrified
and, no, I cannot tell you.

The future is a murky lake.
I am afraid of the monsters
who wait just below its surface.
Even in our mahogany bed, I am not safe.
Each day, I swim toward
everything I didn't want to know.

The Ghosts in Our Bed

The mahogany four-poster bed your mother left us
is high up off the floor. It folds us into
the smell of lavender in sheets sprinkled with violets,
the thick blue and green comforter.
For years we are happy in it,
lusty and young and so alive together,
this safe place to which we return each night
to lie in each other's arms, warm
and exactly where we want to be.

Now, when we climb into our bed, those people
who for so many years were ourselves,
the ghosts that we live with, sleep between us.

You have become so fragile. You are always
cold and need extra blankets, and you sleep
so quietly, your arms folded across your chest,
that when I wake up in the night, I have to reach out
to find you because I'm not certain you're there.
You used to take up so much space, with your energy
and strength, the big bones of your body,
I pile blankets on you now,
your face rigid and frozen even in sleep.
The ghosts of the future hover over us, reminding us
every night of how much more we have to lose,
even as our old ghosts whisper, "Remember, remember."
I fall asleep with my hand on your shoulder,
to keep you with me as long as I can.

Love Poem to My Husband II

I start past you in the hall, rushing, as usual,
to my job or a poetry reading or the post office.
Your face softens when you see me,
and you reach out, saying, "Oh, Maria,
I'm so happy I have you,"
and you gather me into your arms.
"I had a bad dream," you say.
"I dreamt I lost you."

You, who so rarely
put your feelings into words,
startle me with your need.
I watch you when you're sleeping,
your face sad and vulnerable,
your age showing clearly.
This illness that is turning the world around
causes deep crevices and furrows in your face.
You always looked so young.
Often I worried that I looked so much older than you,
but, now, I see your stiff walk,
the bent curve of your back,

one clawed hand trailing behind you like a starched scarf.
Your handwriting shrinks until it is so small
it is almost impossible to read.
Even your voice grows softer, and you speak
as though the space your voice
occupies were vanishing.

I hold you now in the hallway,
try with my strength
and the heat of my body
to save you.

Poem to My Husband of Thirty-Three Years

Love, I wish I could be angry with you for leaving, when I need you here. You aren't even leaving all at once: instead you seem to grow smaller, thinner with each day, your eyes, baffled. You take up less and less space; I want to hate you for the way you're disappearing. Your voice grows softer, so I have trouble hearing you and have to ask you to repeat yourself. Your walk has become so silent, I am often startled to find you behind me, as though you are becoming a ghost, parts of you pared away. Even the air doesn't move when you move. Sometimes when I come into the house, I call and call, the house so still I am sure there is no one in it, until you rise up out of your basement room or call out, after what seems like a long time of shouting your name, and I grumble, "It's like living with a dead person."

The past, iridescent and elusive, floats around us while I drag the present, heavy as stone, with me wherever I go.

In My House There Are No Angels

Lately, my house is crammed full of all the things
I cannot say, my arms laden with words
that drag me down, people
pulling at me, with thick ropes
of need, my sister's crippled, pitiful legs,
red and scarred, her knees
so twisted it seems impossible that she will
ever get up again without help.

Sitting next to her hospital bed
that takes up most of her den,
crammed into the chair next to her,
we talk and she says, "I'm afraid,"
and her hands with their
knotted fingers, are so deformed
the fingers move in all directions.

When I hold her hand I can feel
the bones crack, "I'm afraid.
Do you know where Lourdes is?"
She asks. "I hear they have baths
there where people are healed."

I cross the street to my own house,
and you are waiting for me.
You tell me a long slow story,
groping for the words to explain,
and impatience fills me, though I am ashamed of it,
though I want to be the Blessed Virgin
waiting patient as stone,
I am distracted and uneasy, my
eyes shifting away from you even as
I try to force my attention back

to what you are saying, and my eyes
catch on the angels in the big bowl from Sicily

and the plaster angels, and the angels
on the wall but even with a house
full of angels,
there are no angels here,

no angels to give blessing,
no angels to save my sister
no angels that will wave their
magic arms in the air and make
your illness vanish, no angels that
will ease this itch of impatience I feel
when I see you stuck
in the doorway, your feet unable
to carry you through the door,
your body tipping forward and
back, and you not moving.

On TV there is a program
about angels who always have
the answer and who when they solve
a problem, are suffused
with a glowing light and
God's presence is there,

but in our house surrounded
by artists' renditions of angels,
there are none, the air
devoid of light, no angels to save
my sister or you or me,
only the heaviness that never lifts,
my need to shift you through the door,
my seething anger, my secret
foolish hope that one of the angels will

lift itself by magic off the wall
and hold us in her arms and heal us.

In La Casa de las Americas

In La Casa de las Americas last night a life size cardboard cutout of Fidel Castro is propped in the corner. My friend goes up to him, poses, says wouldn't that make a great photograph? The serious old Cuban men look at her, their faces blank and stony. Earlier I tasted the steak, the blood dripping from it; I ate it though I could taste something odd, off about it, like a lot of my life, odd, off, but satisfying and wonderful.

Strange that everything has two sides to it, like my birthday in March. It stopped mattering a long time ago, but when I was twenty-one, it still mattered. Twenty-one meant I could drink legally and a group of us went to Stasney's and had pizza, four of us talking and laughing and drinking legally for the first time when inexplicably I fell into my own loneliness, that cave that is never quite filled. What will happen to us, I think, while I sit in the Paterson Museum staring at the gray floor and rickety tables and the lined pad I am trying to fill. I imagine a young German immigrant woman bending over her loom, her hand moving the shuttle across the loom, the noise of the cotton dust floating around them, the noise so loud it shuts out everything else. The young woman dreams as her hand moves the shuttle back and forth, the noise and the movement feed her dreams, perhaps of her love, his hands, and here, in the museum surrounded by the colorful artwork by the children of Paterson, the bright burlap banners they have made, I imagine the ghost of that young woman, and the hundreds of others from so long ago who sweated and struggled and dreamed in the incredible heat and noise of the mill. Are their ghosts here, murmuring behind the display cases filled with minerals and polished stones?

When I woke up yesterday, the first thing I saw was the plant that suddenly had one huge, red tropical blossom on it. It reminds me of sex, the way OKeefe's paintings always do. So much I cannot tell you, such conflict impossible to shape into the order of words, the neatness of them, only inside me, a blossom, like that flower, delicate and passionate, that would take you back to the way you were when I first saw your yellow hair, your voice, smooth and sweet as honey, my heart opening like that flower and the Japanese cherry tree that blossomed miraculously outside my window that May morning forty years ago and the first thing this morning when you approached me, your leg dragging across the hardwood floor, the way you offered Al's letter like a gift, the way you reached in and touched me.

The Black Bear on My Neighbor's Lawn in New Jersey

In my neighbor's front yard where one birch tree casts
its pale shadow over their small, suburban ranch house
and the grass is smooth and freshly mowed,

an enormous black plastic bear stands, its paws
upraised as though ready to attack,
its mouth stretched in a senseless grin.

Every year my neighbors have a garage sale
to get rid of all the knickknacks and fake
country plaques and costume jewelry
and mugs with cutsey sayings on them
that they've accumulated during the year.
Next year maybe they'll try to sell
the fake bear with its weird, cockeyed smile,
and maybe they'll even find someone like themselves
to buy it.

Think of it: this plastic bear
doesn't need the wilderness
to live; it doesnt need food.
Two hundred thousand years from now,
if we let the world survive that long,
the people of the future will find it.
Imagine how confused they'll be
as they try to figure out what use
we could have made of it,
what kind of lives we led.

The River at Dusk

Late afternoon, I drive past the Bunker Hill factories
over the new steel girders of the Sixth Avenue bridge.
Through the glossy, silver webwork, I glimpse
the river curving toward downtown Paterson,
the trees over it stark as burnt matches

against the darkening sky.
How beautiful the city is at this hour.
People caught in glass and metal
drive toward lamplight,
the rough brushstrokes of factories in the background.
The river, peaceful and slow, moves as it has
always moved, and at dusk, the rising moon,
like a Lucite dipper, lifts the dark water
into a momentary, exquisite light.

Laura

Laura with your clear and glowing skin,
your cherry red lipstick and perfect teeth,

in the old home movies, you are riding
a donkey in San Mauro's village square.
Nonna is watching you, her face serious
and composed. The old Neapolitan uncles
in their hand-me-down suits and leathery faces
call you *la Mericana,* their yellowed teeth
showing through wide grins.

You are laughing, showing off
your beautiful straight teeth.
In another frame, you are sitting on the back
of a motorcycle, Carlo sitting in a drivers seat,
with your arm around his waist.

You were the one climbing trees
playing baseball in Santangelo's lot,
roller skating over slate sidewalks
at breakneck speed. You were always running,
prancing, whirling, as though you didn't want
to be caught standing still.

Today, your skin has turned dry and opaque,
your hands twisted. You sit in the wing chair
in your den, a rag soaked in alcohol on your head.
Your feet rest on the ottoman, the bones
so deformed they poke through the skin.

How you loved to dance
in your size five shoes,
your slender calves. How the eyes of men
followed you, with your hourglass figure,
your large dark eyes,
your glorious chestnut hair.

Because Poem for Caroline

Because I saw you in your little pink newborn cap
minutes after you were born,
because you lived in New Jersey when you were a baby,
because I held you every week and we went to restaurants
and you were cradled in your baby carrier while we ate
and I could look and look at you,
because I watched you when your Mamma and Daddy went
    out,
because you snuggled into my neck,
because you are sharp and smart, all energy and pepper,
a quicksilver girl with an open heart,
because you love words,
because you like my riddles,
because you laugh like me,
because I like to talk to you on the telephone,
because I wish I could see you more,
because you kiss me on the telephone, a loud, smacking kiss,
because you love *The Wizard of Oz,*
because you plan what we will do when you visit,
because you remind me of my mother,
because when you are excited you glow like a candle in the
    dark,
because you tell me I have a beautiful voice,
because your voice is like mine,
because you listen to music with your heart and body,
because you love to draw,
because we made stew together,
because when you saw the painting in the Raleigh Art Museum

you said, "Oh how beautiful!" and your face lit up, though
    you were only two years old,
because you are my first, my beautiful, my special girl
I can't wait to hug you who are already nearly five years old

and so sharp and smart, all energy and pepper, such
a quicksilver girl with an open heart.

To My Granddaughter Caroline

"Half of me wants you to stay, Grandma, and the other half wants you to go," you say seriously, looking at me with troubled blue eyes. Earlier you told me that sometimes you felt five years old and sometimes a hundred, and immediately I understand and I also know you are no ordinary five year old, though your parents say don't pay attention she's only five. I realize that maybe on this joint vacation, you find my presence distracting, and I tell Dennis, "I won't go to the aquarium this afternoon. I'll make some phone calls instead," and I send Dennis over to your room and two minutes later a knock at the door, and you are there saying, "I want you to come with us, Grandma," and I say, "No, that's o.k. Caroline. You don't have to want me to come. It's o.k.." You insist as does your father. "She's only five," he says again; but when we get in the elevator your huddle in the corner saying under your breath. "Guilty, I feel guilty," over and over, and I don't know how to comfort you.

To My Grandson Jackson
on His Second Birthday

Already it is your second birthday,
and I hardly know you.
I can count on my fingers
the number of times I have seen you,
remember at Christmas
you with your huge solemn blue eyes,
toddling over to a bag with matchbox toys in it
and lifting one car out at a time,
so carefully, precisely
"Car," you said.
and that seemed to be the only word
you had decided to say.

How quiet and content your father was,
how quiet and contented he still is,
how like him you are.

Now, sometimes I talk to you on the phone.
and you are starting to say words clearly,
to come to the phone without hesitation,
you tell me, "Cho cho" for the subway
you rode on in Washington,
"Chocolate" for the candy I sent you
"Night, night," you say clearly.
What else can you do?
How have you changed?
I cannot imagine, look at pictures
of your father at your age,
wish that I could hold you.

To Jackson on Your Third Birthday

You, with your impish grin,
with your chunky legs,
with your wide feet in sneakers that flash
red lights when you walk,
with your big blue eyes,
with your golden hair,
with your quick mind,
you remind me so much
of your father at your age,
the way you concentrate
on your matchbox toys
when you play
or pull the wooden train
around on its track,

the way you want to watch
the train video over and over,

the way you nearly push
me out of my chair
when I'm trying to play see saw
with you.

Oh such joy in your hurtling body,
the way you run from room
to room, laughing,
squealing,
the way you rush to get away
when I try to grab you,
the way you wiggle
and giggle,
when I kiss the folds of your neck,
the way you take your cars,

out of their plastic case
one by one,
examining each with such care.

Daredevil,
broad shouldered trooper
bursting into your three-year old skin,
in my mind I am hugging you.

My Mother Gave Me Her Ring

My mother gave me her ring before she died. It was the only good ring she ever owned until I made my father buy her a diamond engagement ring for their fiftieth anniversary because she never had one and I knew it was the one thing she wanted and her one regret in life was that my father made her give her ring to Mussolini who promised to put a chicken in every pot in Italy or the Italian version of that promise, a chicken even for the Southern Italians like my father, who were detested by the Northern aristocrats, Mussolini who chanted power to the people so convincingly that my father believed him, at least for awhile, until Hitler showed himself to be what he so terribly was and Mussolini too. My father regretted the donation of my mother's gold wedding ring though it was too late to get it back. They had their fiftieth anniversary party at Scordato's and my mother was thrilled to be going out to dinner, only the second time she'd been out to dinner since she came to America when she was twenty-three, and she said, "Oh, those restaurants. I can cook better than that."

But this time we got her a special dress and took photos of the two of them together and of my mother and father surrounded by their children and grandchildren. The photo is now on my mantle. My mother looks proud and happy and I hope that maybe that moment, the gift of the ring she thought was my father's idea, made up for everything she did without all those Paterson years, the way she wanted so much to make those tenements beautiful, the way she said to us, "Money – you think that will make you happy? If you think that, I didn't teach you anything." My mother gave me the yellow and white filigreed ring she got from her mother when she was a girl and wore my father's new diamond ring on her hand when they went out to visit our aunts and uncles or to a family party. I loved my mother's girlhood ring, ran my hand over its lacy surface, over the smoothness of old, eighteen-karat gold, and after she died, I'd touch the ring, remembering her and what she taught me: to treasure my children and keep them close, and to approach the world with open hands. She was only dead a year when I looked down at my hand and saw the ring had vanished I crawled around that grassy parking area looking for the ring, but it was gone. When I told my daughter, she ran up to her room and came down with a silver ring with a pink stone and slipped it on my finger. "Grandpa found this ring when I was in kindergarten and he gave it to me. I want you to have it," she said, and looking at her, I know what my mother meant when she told me my children were the only treasure that I'd ever need.

Piecework

I was told only your name, saw you
as one half of a stiff, formal photograph
in a mahogany frame. You are looking straight
into the camera's lens, your large eyes
dark and unreadable, your hair drawn back
into a bun. Next to you, your husband,
my grandfather, in a black suit, the collar
of his shirt stiff with starch,
space between you
and your bodies do not touch.

Little facts about you
seep through the scrim of silence
my father pulled around you.
When your mother sent for you,
you came to Philadelphia, lived with her
and your stepfather and their children,
met the man who would become your husband.
In two months, you were married. You were sixteen.
The next year, your first child was born;
then a new baby each year for the next four years.

I ask myself; what else do I know about you?
That your auburn hair was so long that
when you took out your hairpins at night,
it reached your thighs.
When my grandfather saw you for the first time walking
down Christian Street, he decided he was going to marry you.
What else do I know?
Your two-year old daughter disappeared for three days.
You left the other children with a friend and
went to the neighborhood witch. She told you where to find
   her.

You did, but someone had forced her to sit
on top of a hot coal stove, and she was badly burned.

One day my grandfather took you
and the children to New York on the train.
He told you that you were going to visit relatives,
but instead he took you to a ship and forced you
to go back to Italy.

In San Mauro, my grandfather went to his uncle,
the village priest, and asked him for a plot of land
to support his family. His uncle said no;
your husband left for Buenos Aires.
You were six months pregnant.

What else do I know?
My grandfather comes back to Italy
to serve in the Italian army.
While he is there, your seventh child is born;
he goes back to Argentina.
My grandfather never came back.
You heard that he loved another woman,
and had a son.

Grandma. Nonna. I don't know what name
I would have used for you. I never met you.
I piece you together now and you are more
than fifty years dead. Were you terrified when he left you,
promising to send money
that never arrived? How long did it take
for you to realize he'd never come back?
How the old women of the town love
your story. How they chew on it,
sitting in the dusty plaza, their black eyes
missing nothing. They watch you,
twenty-four, still beautiful and alone.

You are lonely, no one to hold you
while you try to keep the family together.
Did you cry or scream at your children
or beat them till they bled? What happened
in Philadelphia? What really happened to your child?

You lived in a man's world,
the men going off to find new lives,
the women and children they left behind,
the ones they sometimes forgot
as your husband forgot you.

I imagine myself inside your skin,
what rage, what sorrow.
Nonna, I wish you had left letters,
a diary, poems. I wish I had known you.
I piece you together from scraps of memory,
the things my father never said,
search for you through my own past,
the woman I have become,
the way you fit inside my shadow,
the way you make me strong.

Daddy, We Called You

"Daddy," we called you. "Daddy,"
when we talked to each other in the street,
pulling on our American faces,
shaping our lives in Paterson slang.

Inside our house, we spoke
a Southern Italian dialect
mixed with English
and we called you Papa

but outside again, you became Daddy
and we spoke of you to our friends
as "my father"
imagining we were speaking
of that *Father Knows Best*
TV character
in his dark business suit,
carrying his briefcase into his house,
retreating to his paneled den,
his big living room and dining room,
his frilly-aproned wife
who greeted him at the door
with a kiss. Such space

and silence in that house.
We lived in one big room –
living room, dining room, kitchen, bedroom,
all in one, dominated by the gray oak dining table
around which we sat, talking and laughing,
listening to your stories,
your political arguments with your friends.
Papa, how you glowed in company light,
happy when the other immigrants

came to you for help with their taxes
or legal papers.

It was only outside that glowing circle
that I denied you, denied your long hours
as night watchman at Royal Machine Shop.
One night, riding home from a date
my middle class, American boyfriend
kissed me at the light; I looked up
and met your eyes as you stood at the corner

near Royal Machine. It was nearly midnight.
January. Cold and windy. You were waiting
for the bus, the streetlight illuminating
your face. I pretended I did not see you,
let my boyfriend pull away, leaving you
on the empty corner waiting for the bus
to take you home. You never mentioned it,
never said that you knew
how often I lied about what you did for a living
or that I was ashamed to have my boyfriend see you,
find out about your second shift work, your broken English.

Today, remembering that moment,
still illuminated in my mind
by the streetlamp's gray light,
I think of my own son
and the distance between us,
greater than miles.

Papa,
silk worker,
janitor,
night watchman,
immigrant Italian,
I honor the years you spent in menial work

slipping down the ladder
as your body failed you

while your mind, so quick and sharp,
longed to escape,
honor the times you got out of bed
after sleeping only an hour,
to take me to school or pick me up;
the warm bakery rolls you bought for me
on the way home from the night shift.

The letters
you wrote
to the editors
of local newspapers.

Papa,
silk worker,
janitor,
night watchman,
immigrant Italian,
better than any *Father Knows Best* father,
bland as white rice,
with your wine press in the cellar,
with the newspapers you collected
out of garbage piles to turn into money
you banked for us,
with your mouse traps,
with your cracked and callused hands,
with your yellowed teeth.
Papa,
dragging your dead leg
through the factories of Paterson,
I am outside the house now,
shouting your name.

ITALIAN WOMEN IN BLACK DRESSES

2004

Black Dresses

I dress now all in black like the old ladies
of my childhood, the old ladies who watched

our movements and reported to our mothers
if we did anything wrong. These women, sitting

on their stoops in their shiny black cotton, their black
stockings rolled down to just below their knees,

their sparse, white hair drawn back into a bun, wisps
of it escaping onto their foreheads.

In the heat of an August afternoon, they sat and fanned
themselves with accordion fans that they held

in their hands and moved back and forth to create
some movement of air. They had big white cotton

handkerchiefs they used to pat away the sweat.
These women kept their eyes on the neighborhood.

They could have told all the secrets of each house,
and on evenings, late, sitting under the grape arbor,

while the men played briscole and the children sat quietly,
They told the secrets whispered among the women,

the secrets they held close to them, these women
who were always there for one another.

When there was illness in the family, they would come
to the door with pots of soup and fresh bread, ready

to help clean the floors or care for the children.
Summer evenings under the grape arbor, the children

heard those stories and they stored them in their hearts,
and the women's whispers and laughter became

the music of a time when the world was small
enough to carry in their hands.

Blessed

Blessed be the moments that remain in our minds years after
they happen, moments like the time when I was sitting
in my mother's lap in the old brown rocker, my sister leaning
against us on the broad arm of the chair, my younger brother
and I caught in the circle of my mother's arm, her body

warm as the wood stove that heated our kitchen, my mother
telling a story about growing up in San Mauro, her voice
soothing and smooth as cream on my skin. My brother's
head rests on my arm as his eyelids flutter and fall against

his cheek, his body going limp with sleep, the four of us
bound together and cradled by my fierce and loving mother.
How warmed we were by her fire, our closeness a warmth
we carry with us even now, more than fifty years later,
When I was leaning over my mother, leaning over the

bed where she was dying, I could hear the stories that
she tried to tell me before she died. When she vomited
black blood into my hand, and died and came back
she told me, "I saw my mother and sisters and they were
in a beautiful garden together. They said it was o.k.
to go now." She held my hand and smiled at me,
a smile so radiant that I thought that she was young
again, the way she was when she rocked us

in her arms. To this day I still hear her
breathing inside me, a place
we will always be together and nothing
to fear, nothing to fear.

Perspectives

When I go back to look at it, when the reporter
takes me back and snaps my picture in front
of our house, the house I lived in until I was eleven,
the two family with the extra family hidden
in the dank cellar where the father got pneumonia

and died, the house seems to have grown smaller in size,
the street, too, small and dirty, soda cans and wrappers
in the gutters. The distance too seems shorter from our
house to Pasquale's corner and Burke's Candy Store
where we got ice cream in coated cardboard containers,

vanilla ice cream packed solid and high over the rim
that we ate with a special wooden spoon on the walk home.
In Ventimiglia's vacant lots we played through summers
chasing butterflies we never caught and playing tag
and hide-and-seek. In that field I learned the only nature

I knew, wild daisies and weeds and black-eyed susans,
the whisper of tall wild grass that hid us,
the freedom of those endless summer days. The field
that was huge and welcoming is covered over now
with asphalt and cement and rows of garages, the earth

plastered over, every inch of it sealed in. The reporter asks
me questions, but my mind is caught in the past, caught
in the scent of Zio Guillermo's garden, the silk tassels
of corn, the dew on the huge tomatoes, the smell of earth
and growing things and Zio Guillermo hiding in the garden

from Zia Concetta's anger. The neighborhood children,
Big Joey, Little Joey, Judy, my sister and brother, gathered
on the back stoop in the summer darkness, telling stories

and smoking punks to keep away the mosquitoes. Often,
in the evenings, my mother would call us inside

and wash us with the stiff washcloths she sewed,
and comb our hair. We'd walk to Aunt Rose's
house to sit under the grape arbor in the evening,
the men playing cards, wine in short glasses before them.

While the men played cards, we sat near the women
who were sipping espresso and talking, listening
to the stories they told till they forgot we were there,
the stories of people we knew or had never met,
stories that come back to me now, tart and sweet,

a taste of mint and sugar, a drop of espresso
in a big cup of milk. Those moments glow
like junk jewelry I buy in thrift stores.
How can I tell this young reporter
what it was like to grow up here?

Her eyes see it as a slum, ratty and poor;
my eyes remember those moments walking home
from Zia Rosa's in the dark, the world soft
and shiny, the stars still visible in the Paterson sky,
the music of stories and words singing in my head.

Holding my brother's hand, I walk ahead of my mother.
I am in love with the evening, the stars, my brother's
hand, the cracked sidewalk, roses climbing fences
and trellises, the vegetables and flowers the immigrants
planted, the stone birdbaths they built, my skin about to burst
in its sweetness, the stories stored up like treasure
that I would find again and again as I grew older.

The Past

The past is a photo album, a collection of still photographs
pasted on black pages, little silver triangles to hold
the pictures in, only these pictures are ones I never took,
pictures of us under Zia Rosa's grape arbor, the grown-ups
sitting around a large oilcloth-covered table, the women
at one end, talking, and the men playing briscole,
wine in short glasses before them.
We watched from the fringes of the group,
the men serious, cigarette smoke rising above
their heads, and the women at the other end
of the table, whispering together about the Riverside
families, their voices soft and happy in the summer air.

The light bulbs strung from the arbor buzzed with insects,
and we, children, listened to the stories our mother's told
to one another, understanding only that they didn't realize
how much we heard. Those evenings, the air heavy
with the perfume of the huge clusters of purple grapes
that grew from the vine, the aroma of corn and tomatoes
from the garden, the contained world where everyone
we loved was together, and today, across the distance
of forty years, I would go back, take a photograph
of those evenings, my father's face jovial, his hooked nose,
his clean clear skin, his love of company and politics,
and my shy mother, still young, sexy in her black
mourning dress, her hair shining under the light
of that dangling bulb, her reserve broken
by the company of other women, and the stories
they told, my brother, sister, and I listening
to their voices and drinking cream soda.
I would capture these moments if I could,
my mother, father, Zio Gianni, Zia Rosa,
Zio Guillermo, Zia Louisa, all dead now,

the only thing remaining to pass on to my children
is this memory that when I, too, die,
will have vanished forever, as the world I grew
up in has already vanished and not even
a photograph to show what once was.

After School on Ordinary Days

After school on ordinary days we listened
to *The Shadow* and *The Lone Ranger*
as we gathered around the tabletop radio
that was always kept on the china cabinet
built into the wall in that tenement kitchen,
a china cabinet that held no china, except
thick and white and utilitarian,
cups and saucers, poor people's cups
from the 5 & 10 cents store.
My mother was always home
from Ferraro's Coat factory
by the time we walked in the door
after school on ordinary days,
and she'd give us milk with Bosco in it
and cookies she'd made that weekend.
The three of us would crowd around the radio,
listening to the voices that brought a wider world
into our Paterson apartment. Later

we'd have supper at the kitchen table,
the house loud with our arguments
and laughter. After supper on ordinary
days, our homework finished, we'd play
monopoly or gin rummy, the kitchen
warmed by the huge coal stove, the wind
outside rattling the loose old windows,
we inside, tucked in, warm and together,
on ordinary days that we didn't know
until we looked back across a distance
of forty years, would glow and shimmer
in memory's flickering light.

Sunday Mornings

Sunday mornings my father bought crumb buns on his way
home from the night shift at Royal Machine Shop. My mother

didn't believe in laziness so she'd get us out of bed at seven
and send us off scrubbed and neat to the nine o'clock

children's mass at Blessed Sacrament Church. We still fasted
then before mass. We'd walk down 2nd Avenue and up

the 16th Street hill to the old brick church with its long row
of cement steps and its big carved wooden door

and into the high ceremony of its flickering candles,
the geometry of its vaulted ceilings, the dim,

incense laden interiors, the bruised, bearded face of Jesus
on his cross, the smooth dark wood of the pews. In that

mysterious interior, I was lost in a country that buzzed with
meaning, a place where I could let the solemn organ music

that strained toward the heavens, the fluttery voices
of the choir, fill me. In my head I'd make up songs

and stories while the priest's voice rose and fell
intoning the Mass in his strange and lovely Latin,

chanting and ringing his altar bells. Later,
we'd walk home together. My mother

and father would be in the kitchen where the aroma
of meatballs and tomato sauce pulled us in, my mother

cooking Sunday dinner, the tomato sauce and meatballs
simmering in the pot, the chicken and potatoes ready

to be placed in the oven. On the table, there was always
a white bakery bag of crumb buns. The aroma

of the freshly baked buns mingled with the smell
of my mother's cooking. I picked the huge crumbs

off the top of the buns and ate the bun itself last,
smiling at my father who had been waiting for the smile,

each of us circling around those buns, joking and laughing.
My father would sit reading the Italian paper. We'd play

dominoes or start a game of monopoly while we waited
for my mother to serve dinner. We always ate at noon

on Sunday so we could go out in the afternoon to visit
our aunts and cousins, but Sunday mornings were quiet

and sacred. We'd circle around my mother pestering her
for a meatball, not wanting to wait for twelve

which seemed an eternity away. My mother gave us each
a meatball and tomato sauce in a saucer along with hot

bread with butter. We'd go back to listening to the radio
or playing our games. Do I imagine that the air of that time

seems to shine soft and silken?

My First Room

Had no carpet, instead inexpensive linoleum
that had to be rolled out on the floor

after my father carted it home from the store
in his arms. The room was unheated.

The windows froze over with ice crystals
in elaborate lace patterns all winter.

The loose-fitting windows rattled
and moaned in the wind. It had

no closet, the assumption being
that people poor enough to live

in this room wouldn't own enough clothes
to need a closet. And without electrical outlets

there could be no lamp to soften the rough edges.
My first room had a three-quarter bed

that I shared with my sister Laura. It was gunmetal
gray and ugly like the kind of bed used in institutions.

We had a small bureau with three small drawers.
The room was tiny; there was barely enough room

for the bureau and bed. We had to slide in sideways
to climb into the bed with its white chenille spread.

When I was thirteen, my mother bought a pink-shaded lamp
that clipped onto the headboard. Under the glow of that lamp,

I read *Mill on the Floss, Tess of the D'Urbervilles, Jude the Obscure.* In those books, I was carried to other

places that caught and held my imagination and taught me the power of language to make even the darkest place beautiful.

Gym Class

When I was still a skinny little kid in PS18,
Mrs. Day, our gym teacher, was very tough

looking and athletic. Her freckled face, deeply tanned
even in winter, didn't smile. She'd stand, her hands

on her hips, shouting commands, her legs
with their hard-looking calves positioned,

ready for battle on that polished wooden floor.
I entered the gym, having dressed cautiously,

trying to use the locker doors as a screen.
I was afraid to look at anyone else and hoped

that no one was looking at me. I'd step into
that blue cotton gym suit that needed to be ironed

every time we had gym. It had elastic around the legs
and pants that ballooned out from the elastic at the waist

to the elastic around the tops of our legs. My gym suit
was passed down from my sister who was chunky and

developed early, the elastic was all stretched out and droopy,
the blue was faded from being washed so much. In winter,

we'd have class inside the gym, some children, sleek
and coordinated and loving the opportunity to run

and jump and show off, and some children, like me,
uncoordinated and bookish, incapable of doing

most of the things Mrs. Day required us to do.
I particularly hated the leather horse

we were supposed to jump over. It seemed
very high to me. Mrs. Day would line us all up.

Each person in turn would run toward the horse
while the others watched. We were supposed

to vault over the horse without tripping
or falling on the other side. Many,

or so it seemed to me, accomplished
this feat with ease. Each time, as I waited

my turn I'd think it looked easy.
I hoped that while watching the others

I'd learn the secret of leaping over the horse.
I'd run toward the horse, make a feeble pass

at vaulting over it. I'd end up standing there
as though I'd run into a wall. "I can't do it,"

I'd say, but Mrs. Day would shout, "Try again."
I'd get about twelve inches off the ground and fall

back again, unable to get to the other side
of the horse I'd grown to hate. Everyone

watched. Finally, Mrs. Day would give up
and let me off the hook. Every day

I was confronted with tasks my awkward body
couldn't accomplish. "Climb the rope," Mrs. Day

would shout. My eyes would follow the rope
to the ceiling. I'd try, but these skills were ones

that would elude me my whole life. I was perfect
at missing the ball when I'd try to swing at it. After years

of failing at athletic pursuits, I knew before I began
that I couldn't manage the trick of coordination

that it took to be good at these skills. I wonder if the kids
who weren't good at school, the ones who continually got F

instead of A in their work, felt as hopeless as I did
when confronted by that leather horse, or a baseball

speeding toward me as I held the bat
as far away from me as I could.

Kitchen

We ate in the 17th Street kitchen with its scrubbed
oilcloth, its strong, plain wooden table and chairs,

enough for all of us and for all the aunts and uncles
who joined us at Sunday dinners that my mother cooked

on the big iron coal stove with its polished chrome.
She served dinner on the thick, ugly dishes

from the five and ten cent store that she lifted down
from the glass-fronted cabinet built into the wall, served

the spaghetti and meatballs and *bracciola* steaming
to the table, and my father poured short glasses of wine

for each adult and water with a drop or two of wine
for each child. We were expected to be silent

in that big kitchen with its tin ceiling while the grown-ups
gossiped and laughed, taking turns, it seemed to me then,

in telling stories, arguing politics, their Italian words
floating around my head, soft as a cashmere

shawl, the music of their words, the way it warms me
even today to hear that softness and the beauty of Italian

fill a room, the language that I taught myself not to use.
I can still see that classroom at Eastside High school.

Mrs. Pennyroyal with her delicate intonations,
looking out at us in sophomore year and telling us

that anyone who spoke another language at home
and thought in that language, would score 100 points lower

on the SAT than those who did not. I was sure
she was speaking to me, that I was the only one, though

looking back now I wonder how many others in that gray
room felt the same flush of shame rise in their cheeks.

How many others learned that day to erase their family's
words and force themselves to think in English, denying

themselves the lilt of their first language, the language
of their hearts. I see us sitting under light of that dangling

bulb in my mother's kitchen, the inexpensive glass shade
unable to soften the light. I see the linoleum clean

and buffed to a shine, though worn through in spots
and ugly, the coal stove crackling, the entire table,

my mother, father, sister, brother, my aunts and uncles
coated by memory in a wash of silver light. Italian words

ring in my head, an unrepentant joy that I reclaim
and hold to my face, as if the words were a rose

and I could put my nose to the flower
and inhale its glorious, unforgettable perfume.

Taking a Risk

When I was eleven, I decided
I needed to be punished
for my sins. If I could
expiate them, I would get everything
my heart desired, and that was a lot.

I went out into the parking area
of the Riverside Presbyterian Church,
and dropped to my bare, scabbed knees
and walked across the stones, gray
and chunky, larger than gravel and pointier.

I'd walk around on my knees, the stones
digging into them, and I'd chant prayers
hoping to transform my life.

Years later, in Portugal, at Our Lady of Fatima
shrine, I saw people walking on their knees
on paving stones. Some of them cheated
and wore foam rubber pads on their knees;
some wrapped handkerchiefs around them.
The tourists stared. The penitents
held their rosaries in their hands,
their eyes lifted toward heaven,

but when I saw them, I was reminded
of my eleven-year-old self, those moments
when I walked on my knees, chanting
"Hail Mary, Full of Grace," and pretending
that I was looking for something I'd lost
in case any of the neighbors were watching.
At eleven I was practical so I only did it
a few times and gave it up when it didn't work,

From this distance, I want to comfort
the child I was and the ghost of that child
who still lives inside me, sharing that common
guilt we carry for sins we cannot name.

Halloween Costumes

When I was twelve and in seventh grade Diane Vanderwende,
one of the few Dutch kids in our class where most of us
were Italian, decided to have a Halloween party
at her house on River Street. Her mother, doll-like

and pretty, looked very American. She made a costume
for Diane, a real costume made from material she bought
at the store. Diane was dressed as a woman in a harem
with a slinky costume with sheer black pants

which ballooned out and were fastened at the ankles
with gold straps. She wore gold and black shoes with bells
on the tip-tilted toes and a tight fitting top. Her midriff
was bare. Her bolero jacket covered her breasts and had
filmy black veiling formed into sleeves with gold bands

at the wrists and a slit, so her arms were visible under the veils.
The costume was perfect, Diane looked beautiful with her
creamy magnolia skin, her deep black hair and her big
blue eyes. My mother made a costume for me to wear,
but she couldn't afford to buy material, so she used
old net curtains. I didn't know what it was supposed to be.
I suspect that my mother didn't either.
She fastened the netting in layers at my waist and made a

shawl to cover my shoulders and a scarf for my head
made up of the same faded white net which made my skin
look green-tinged and sickly. "I'm a peasant woman," I said
when someone asked. I wasn't sure what a peasant woman

was supposed to look like. The netting was itchy.
I spent the night feeling awkward and embarrassed.
When Diane's mother offered me a piece of birthday cake,

a store bought confection made with whipped cream,
I, who was thin because I didn't like food,

especially American food, and never tried anything new
if I could help it, said, "No, thank you, I'm allergic to it."
Diane's mother and her aunts laughed and kept repeating,
"I'm allergic to it," as if it were the funniest thing
they had ever heard. Diane took every opportunity

to walk around the room, showing off her exquisite
costume. I huddled in the darkest corner
waiting until it was time to go home.

I Want to Write a Love Poem

I want to write a love poem for the big-eyed girl I was in seventh grade and for Joe Rogers and his American good looks, for his eyes, bright and deep as willow pattern china. He always tried to protect me, as though I were fragile and needed his gestures, extravagant as Sir Walter Raleigh's flung cape. He walked me home from school past Warner Piece Dye Works and the weedy cracks in the sidewalk, past Cuccinello's candy store where neither of us could afford to stop.

I want to write a love poem for Joe Rogers who was beaten every night by his drunken father. I'd hear the whoosh of the belt and the harsh slap hit his back. After what seemed like forever, I'd hear him cry out. That cry was what his father waited for, and the belt would cease its terrible arc. Next morning, together we'd retrace our path to the school. We both pretended I didn't know.

I want to write a love poem for Joe Rogers and the way he made me feel, though we never said the word love, never kissed. In my mind he had full and feathered angel's wings that would have protected me from all that was soiled in the world around us.

I want to write a love poem for Joe Rogers who, that year, moved out with his family in the middle of the night and never came back. No one knew where they had gone. I never had a chance to say goodbye. I'd like to tell him how I hope he escaped a father's legacy passed on to him with each drunken slap.

I want to write a love poem for Joe Rogers and thank him for the tenderness he taught me. I want to tell him I hope he found in our shy and whispered conversations comfort for the soreness of his wounds.

Parties

Looking back, I remember three parties
but they really could be the same party

because I was always confused, a half beat behind
everyone else, innocent in some out-of-it way

that made people, even when I was a young woman,
want to protect me. Partially I think it was my big dark eyes,

my wild hair that refused to be anything but the frizzy
hair of someone thoroughly foreign and young.

When I see pictures of Renaissance women, I see myself,
my long thin face, that Mediterranean look.

I was always reading, escaping into the world of books
that seemed so much more beautiful and alive

than the world of 19th Street, with its tilted cement
front porch that went right up to the curb and Warner

Piece Dye Works across the street. I remember a party
in seventh grade at Ralphie Corollo's house on 18th Street.

We played spin the bottle. When the bottle pointed toward me,
I was awkward and embarrassed. I went into a corner to kiss
Richie, Nick, or Joe. Most of the time I turned my head
just as they were about to kiss me, and their kiss

landed on my cheek or eyebrow. I had a hard time
figuring out what to do with my nose. If the kiss

did hit its mark on my lips, I didn't know what to do
or what I was supposed to feel. At twelve years old,

I felt nothing, though I wanted to desperately.
I think of last month at the poetry reading

when Gerald Stern, whom I had just introduced,
turned to kiss me and tried to kiss me on the lips,

and I turned away. His kiss landed on my cheek.
He went up to the microphone and said,

"Don't you hate it when you try to kiss a woman
on the lips and she turns away?" he said. I was hurled

back to seventh grade, those kisses in corners, the way
I never know what to do in social situations,

though I am old now and should know. That little
girl in Ralph's living room lives inside me,

awkward and inept; she comes out
just when I think she's finally disappeared.

Magic Circle

My mother drew her magic circle around us, led us inside
where we were always safe. She told us stories,
spinning the thread back between herself and her mother
and her mother's mother and connecting that thread to us
her daughters and teaching us how to connect

the same thread to our daughters and granddaughters,
all those women baking bread and bearing children,
teaching us to love ourselves, love them. The stories,
save our lives, passing the meaning on from one
generation to the next, a silver thread, a silver

thread that strengthens us, all those women,
caught in our hearts, teaching us how to laugh,
how to make our arms into cradles
to hold each other and sing.

My First Date

My first date was with Herman Westfall. I was twelve
years old and in seventh grade. I asked him to a dance

at the YWCA. It was a Sadie Hawkins dance. He said "no"
Not a soft "no," but a loud explosive one. He leaped back,

as though I had hit him. Herman Westfall was a skinny
little Dutch boy who went to the Lutheran Church

on Madison Avenue. Later, his family would move out
of Paterson to Wyckoff, a safe, neat, upper-middle-class

suburb to get away from us, the immigrant Italians
who crowded into Paterson and who had no idea why

so many FOR SALE signs went up all around them
as soon as they moved in. I asked Herman

because he seemed the least threatening of all the boys
in our class, certainly not sophisticated as Mikey Russo,

or tough as Joey Calsorre, or street-wise as Richie Serbo.
I was sorry for Herman when Mrs. Elmer hit him

with the ruler in second grade, WHACK! the ruler
would go. Whack! Whack! and I would feel I was being hit

instead. Anyway, I asked him and he said "no." He sat behind
me. I turned around fast, his No! a slap on my face.

I spent the rest of the morning with the blackboard
swimming before me. At recess, Judy asked me

what was wrong, and I told her. She rushed off to tell
the other girls. Soon they crowded around me.

I said it didn't matter, but no one believed me. Later,
Herman tapped me on the shoulder and told me

he would take me to the dance. I don't remember
the dance, or the dress I wore, or how

we got to the Y on Broadway, or who picked us up.
I do remember my shame that he had to be forced

to take me. I cringe at my twelve-year-old self,
too shy to say no back to him, to accept

instead the crumbs the girls in the class forced skinny
Herman Westfall to give, pale, anemic Herman Westfall

with nothing to recommend him but his corn silk-hair.

Cafeteria

In the cafeteria at Eastside High School there was a sour
milk smell that slapped my face when I stepped through

the door. A line of kids circled the room waiting to get
their food. The cafeteria ladies, plump and wearing hair

nets, doled out macaroni and cheese and hamburgers. I
sat at a table with the others who brought their lunch

from home, pulling out my garlicky-smelling escarole
sandwich, or pizza *chiana* or some other Italian delicacy,

and ate shyly in little bites hoping no one would notice
the sharp tang of garlic in the air. Then the voices and

clanking trays and boys clowning with one another to
get the girls' attention rose to a high-pitched roar after

a few minutes, and the cafeteria monitors, teachers
forced to take turns patrolling, blew their whistles.

I usually sat with two or three girls who were
my friends and we would talk and laugh together

quietly. We tried to eat fast and get out. The cafeteria
terrified us. Fights broke out regularly and boys, you

know the kind, loud and teetering on some invisible line
between crazy and just plain brash, would decide

to hound someone, especially someone frightened or
vulnerable. One day three of these boys, they seemed

to be huge to me in retrospect, saw us walking out
of the cafeteria, and one of them in an out of control

manic rage yelled at me, "You're so ugly!
Why don't you get your nose done?" His face screwed up

with disgust, and I cowered away from him, my eyes
filling with tears, his friends laughing, my friends indignantly

walking away from him, telling me not to mind him.
"What a jerk he is!" they said, but I knew that they were

relieved that he had picked on me and not them, all of us,
small and fragile, so unsure, the least breath

could change us forever.

In the Stacks at the Paterson Public Library

When I was fourteen, I asked my father to help me get a job. He called the mayor and asked him for help. My father had worked very hard to get out the vote; so the mayor owed him a favor. When my father said I wanted a job in the Paterson Public Library, the Mayor said, "But that pays only 50 cents an hour." My father told me, and I said I still wanted to work in the library. I loved to read, loved the branch library, loved the feel of a book in my hands. I went off to the Public Library where I was told to speak to Ms. Cherry, Supervisor of Circulation. I went there after school, walked from Eastside High to the imposing white columned library, through the marble hall with its curving stair and bronze statues and oil paintings donated by the wealthy old families of the city. Ms. Cherry gave me a sour look, sniffed, and told me quickly what to do; I knew she wasn't happy that I had been palmed off on her and she let me know she didn't like it.

Another young woman started the same day, a tall, beautiful, light-skinned African-American who came from an upper-middle class family. Her father owned a funeral home. She had expensive clothes and straight hair. We both loved books and we liked to talk to each other in the stacks. She knew Ms. Cherry hated us both, but this girl, her name was Anthea, was more articulate and confident than I was. I was incredibly shy and tongue-tied but she'd answer Ms. Cherry back or give her a look that would shut her up immediately. Then Ms. Cherry would scowl at me and find something wrong with what I'd done. She'd yell, and tears would fill my eyes. "Never let her see you cry," Anthea said. "It just makes her happy."

Despite Ms. Cherry, I liked the job, carrying books up into the stacks on the translucent thick glass stairs. Five floors of stacks lined with books. I'd rush up the stairs and shelve the books so I could read for five or ten minutes. Mostly poetry books by

Amy Lowell, Edna St. Vincent Millay, Elinor Wylie, e.e. cummings. Light cascading through the stacks, the transparent floors, and onto the poems that soared inside of me, the words seemed to take wing against everything gray and ordinary in my life.

One day Ms. Cherry accused me of stealing a book by Shakespeare. It was missing from where it belonged. Suddenly, all my outrage at the way she treated me, the disdainful way she always spoke to me, rose up, and shy mouse of a girl, I turned on her, my eyes flashing fire. My voice rose so everyone in the library heard, and I said, "I do not steal books and don't ever accuse me of doing something like that again!" my shoulders flung back, my eyes saying if she didn't take it back I'd slug her. She said "I'm sorry. I'm sorry. Of course you didn't. I don't know what I was thinking," and Anthea, standing behind us, flashed me a huge victory grin.

The Bed I Remember

The metal bed, not the beautiful iron beds
with the handmade quilts that are so popular today,
but the gray metal bed that we had, the one I slept in
with my sister, while we were in that 17th Street apartment
in Paterson, the bed where my sister peed on me
every night, the bed with its clean cotton sheets

that my mother washed in the wringer washer everyday
and hung out in the sun to dry so they smelled of fresh
air and were so cool against my cheeks, the bed where I read
all the novels I loved with characters far removed
from my 17th Street house and my sister

and the damp cold feel of the wet sheets
when I woke up in the morning and the way
we never talked about it, the wet sheets
or my sister's problem, though after a while
I didn't think about it anymore,

until when I was thirteen and we went to the shore
for the first time, to Long Branch, a boarding house,
with my aunts and grown cousins and my mother washed
the sheets out by hand in the claw-footed tub and hung them
out the window to dry, the sheets a flag that said someone
in that room wet the bed. I was ashamed of the waving
and flapping of the wet sheets in the strong breeze
from the ocean, ashamed in front of the other
city kids who congregated on the driveway to play stickball
and tag in the summer dusk, ashamed for my sister, sixteen
already, and still wetting the bed and the way we never
mentioned it. Just the way today, we pretend we don't see
the cracks in each other's lives, the secrets we both know
but will never tell. My mother trained us to carry our own

burdens, to keep our secrets to ourselves, and we have
carried them until they were so heavy we thought we'd die,

our mouths sealed shut by everything we were afraid to say,
afraid that if we started we'd never stop, as deliberately blind
as we were when those sheets flapped in the Long Branch
wind and we pretended we did not see them.

What I Didn't Learn in School

I didn't learn geometry,
Except for the shortest distance
Between two points
Is a straight line.
The rest was a blur
Through which I stumbled,
Confused and uncertain,
My mind tuning out
When poor bald-headed
Mr. McGinn tried to explain
Geometry to all the Alpha class
Math students who caught on
Right away.

Mr. McGinn was going to fail me
That first semester. I walked up to his desk,
Held out my report card, the marks
All written in neat black fountain-pen ink,
And his head snapped up in shock.
On my report card my marks, 95,
100, 95, 100, 100, 100.
"Is this your report card?" He asked,
And I saw his pen hesitate
While he thought it over.
Slowly, he wrote in a 75.
I went back to my desk, knowing
I didn't deserve to pass,
But knowing too that nothing
Would make me learn geometry,
Not Mr. McGinn with his big, shiny head,
Not the pity in his blue eyes
When he looked at me.
He never called on me again.

I did the homework each night,
Struggling to understand,
And for the first time, I knew
What it was like for those kids
Who always had trouble in school.

I was an Alpha kid, and we were
The brightest kids in the school.
Our classes were held on the third floor,
A symbol that we deserved the top floor.
How humiliating, then, to watch
The other Alpha kids learn
All those angles and lines
Without effort.
I sat, still as a beaten dog,
Tears trembling in my eyes,
While I tried to wrap my mind
Around theorems
But always failed.

Dorothy

Dorothy, you wore pale powder blue that 1950s color
that set off your light blonde hair, every day
a different cashmere sweater set, a little pullover
that came to your waist and was covered by a matching
cardigan in pale blue with little mother of pearl buttons.

You wore the sweater unbuttoned, the sweater underneath
showing through, and at your neck, a string of small pearls.
Your hair, so clean and thick, fell to your shoulders, straight
but curled under in a page boy. You were the Class Secretary,

bubbly and popular; you were always with Charlie, the Class
President. I see you standing in the hall with him after classes.
You are leaning against the wall, his handsome face close
to yours. When he smiles my insides shake, but of course,

he sees only you with your thick wool skirt, and bobby socks,
you with your easy laughter, Charlie destined for great
things, and you the most popular girl, destined to be his,
with your straight white teeth, your delicate features,
your big blue eyes. I watched you from a distance,
saw the way you cut a charmed path
through Eastside High School. Voted "Mr. & Mrs. Eastside,"
you smile from our polished yearbook pages. You look

like people who are sure to inherit the earth, and I,
on the sidelines, watch you, conscious of where I am
in relation to you that I cannot even envy you, know nothing
could transform my immigrant face, my unruly dark hair,
my long nose, my clothes that are always all wrong.
I want only to watch the light that shines around you,
to touch, for one moment, a shimmering I can never own.

Bed

When my daughter was about eight years old, I bought her a white four-poster canopy bed, living out some fantasy of little girlhood that was leftover from my childhood when I shared a brown metal bed with my sister. I loved my sister, admired her because she was so beautiful and lively, a daredevil who climbed trees and played baseball and ran off with my cousin Philip and his friends, while I lay on our bed reading novel after novel, and dreaming.

When we were older my mother replaced that brown metal bed with a maple bed from Maiella's furniture store, but the room was still so small, you had to sidle around it sideways. The bed and dresser matched and it was always so clean, it practically leaped up and shouted, the way those towels on TV do, and the bed, that metal bed that I shared with my sister, was a raft that carried me far away from that lopsided Paterson house with its big kitchen, its wood-burning stove, the squares of linoleum, the oilcloth covered table, the miniscule bedroom painted with paint that was on sale because the colors were so putrid, Pepto-bismol pink or lemon yellow, and it was in that bedroom that I read *Silas Marner* and *Emma* and *The Way of All Flesh* and *Jane Eyre,* those books that made me fall in love with stories and words. I always loved my sister who let me snuggle my skinny body against hers and let me tag along with her friends when I didn't have any of my own. Yet I still wanted my daughter to have what I did not – the spacious room, the matched curtains and bedspread and canopy, the delicate carved spindles on the bed, the warmth of sitting on her bed, reading stories to her, imagining for her a life, easier and more beautiful than my own, not knowing, then, how I'd learn to look back at those years on 19th Street and see them through a scrim of silver light, see them as the treasure I'd try to recreate in poems and stories I'd hand to my daughter trying to give her something more lasting than canopy beds to pass on.

Going to the Movies

When I was still young, movie theaters were opulent palaces,
heavy with maroon velvet draperies and candelabras, ornate
carvings and crystal chandeliers. We went as often
as we could to the Fabian or the Rivoli,
losing ourselves in the flickering world of the screen

In the dark of the theater, we learned
that there were people in the world
whose lives were fur-lined and comfortable, their houses
large and elegant, their expensive cars smelling of leather
and perfume. Strangely, I don't think it mattered to us,

not then, because these people with their affected
accents were so removed from our 17th Street world,
our Italian family, our kitchen table covered in scrubbed
oilcloth and our coal stove, that we regarded them
as foreign creatures inhabiting a world

we knew we couldn't live in since we'd never fit in,
but we could visit it for a while in these movies,
grateful to have seen it, but glad to return
to Main Street and to walk together to Burke's
Ice Cream Parlor, if we had the money, or just
to the bus stop to ride home if we didn't.
Even today, though we rarely go the movie theater anymore,
when I enter a theater and sit in the mysterious dark,
I am pulled into the flickering world
in a way I never am when I'm watching the VCR.
Once we took my mother to the movies when we were
teenagers. My mother objected and complained,

said she didn't have time for such nonsense, sitting straight
as a yardstick in her chair, wearing one of the few better

dresses she owned. We never asked her to go with us again, because she resisted the idea and acted angry, but when she was dying at seventy-eight, she asked me

if I remembered the day we went to the movies, the only movie she ever saw. "It was so nice," she said, and she smiled. "But, Ma, you said you didn't like it!" " Oh what do you know? I was happy to be there with you! It was nice," she whispered, and held my hand till she fell asleep.

Learning to Sing

I am in the hallway of the 19th Street house. The front door is a double door. One side is always kept locked, the other side opens when you turn a deadbolt. The door is painted dark brown, a color that is also used for the floor, the banister, and stairs to the upstairs apartment, the door to our apartment. Usually we use the back door into the kitchen, but today I have gone out to get the mail and see a letter for me. I stand in the hallway to open the letter that looks official and is embossed with a return address that says Seton Hall University. The letter is addressed to me.

The letter tells me I have been awarded a full four-year scholarship to Seton Hall University in Paterson, and this scholarship covers four full years of tuition. I shout for my mother, am excited to have won the award. We make so much noise in the hallway that the people upstairs look down to find out what happened.

Suddenly, with my family around me, I realize that I will have to take this scholarship, that I won't be going to the University of Virginia, as I had hoped with its colonnades and old brick and ivy. I had imagined it, though I had not been out of Paterson more than three times in my life, and had no idea what the University of Virginia represented, the kind of people who went there, the way I would have been awkward and out of place. At least, I will not have to go to William Paterson College to major in Kindergarten or first grade teaching as my mother would like. Instead, I can go to Seton Hall, major in English, dream of becoming a writer. When I announce my ambition, my cousin Joey, the accountant, says it's the most impractical thing he's ever heard.

My mother used to say, "Your fate waits behind the door. You cannot see it, but it is there." In that hallway, behind that brown door, my fate came to me: to stay in Paterson, to go to college a few blocks from Eastside High School, to absorb the feel of the city for four more years, to carry the voice of its people, my people, in my head, to hear their stories, and save them to tell. The voices rise in my head, insistent, wanting to be heard, stories they could never have told, never have found the words to tell them. In my stories, I hear these people who are so much a part of my life, their voices caught like music in my mind. I had to cry a long time before I could learn to sing their songs, my own.

My Mother Who Could Ward Off Evil

My lucky dress has disintegrated, the underslip, patched with
tape that won't hold for long, and the fabric begins to tear.
I am afraid to be without it, even tattered as it is, that
superstitious belief that I can be saved by wearing this dress,
the same way I was sure, when I was a little girl
and you pinned a scapula and an evil eye horn
to my undershirt, that these magic charms could protect
me from all harm. For years, I was afraid to go anywhere
without them, even when I graduated from an undershirt
to a bra, but I think that you were connected
to those talismans, you were the rabbit's foot that protected
me from harm, you were the one, the marvel
that kept me warm, the hands that soothed and healed.
In the kitchen where you baked bread
and the aroma filled that apartment, I was safe

from the world outside that you taught me not to trust,
the world where all the universe of evil could get at me
and you, in your homemade apron, you with flour
on your hands, you serving bowls of steaming food,
you canning tomatoes and peaches, you chopping
wood for the stove, you could not protect me,
and in your fear, I learned my own, needing something
like a lucky dress to keep me safe as I walked
through all the dangerous, exciting places my life
would take me, the places where you could not follow.

I carry your memory with me wherever I go, and understand
only now that you wanted the scapula and evil eye horn
to give me courage, so that they would make me brave,
when you could no longer be there waiting for me
in your warm kitchen, your arms open,
your eyes welcoming me home.

My Father Always Bought Used Cars

My father always bought used cars. They usually collapsed into a heap five days after he bought them. He was always having them repaired. One day he went off with a friend to buy another used car. The blue and white Chevy that he had was a disaster; he had to pay to have it taken away. We heard him pull into the driveway in the new used car, and rushed to the window to see, the car, a bright red Dodge, with two doors, a sporty model that looked like a young man's car. My father was sixty-two at the time, already retired from the factory, his leg dragging and weaker than ever. My mother was horrified. "What will people think?" she said in Italian, "A bright red car!" My mother was shy, hated to call attention to herself, thought this red car crass and flamboyant, like waving a flag to say, "Here I am." My mother was angry at my father for buying the red car and went around grumbling for years about it, calling him names under her breath as she cooked and cleaned. Maybe she was afraid that the car would bring envy down on us: I don't know. I do know that she never got into or out of the car without complaining. Everyone in town knew my father. He drove, his hands clutching the wheel, his back stiff, at a maximum speed of ten miles an hour. More often, he kept the speedometer at five miles an hour. He was always in first gear. Our cat got to know when he was coming. My father would inch around the corner from Kingston onto Oak and the cat would come running from wherever he was. My father brought treats for the cat – liver and fish – and the cat knew him and would follow him wherever he went, its tail wagging. My mother, who thought cats were dirty beasts who shouldn't be allowed inside, chased the cat with the broom, cursing him in Italian, when she saw the cat sitting on the sofa. When it saw her coming into the house, the cat would hide and wouldn't come out for hours.

Cheap

Cheap – the clothes I wore when I was in grammar school
and high school, cheap and not quite right.
Imitation blue jeans that weren't blue but black,
so everyone knew they weren't the right kind.

Cheap – the nylon see-through blouse I wore in high school,
white against my sallow skin making me look jaundiced,
sleazy nylon that felt strange and synthetic to the touch,
and the plain white cotton slip underneath
with its fake edging of cheap lace.

Cheap – the dresses we made for graduation from PS18,
white eyelet lace, scratchy and stiff, not soft like expensive
lace. The dresses with their little cap sleeves were tight
over the bodice to the nipped in waist, my sewing ability
so poor that my mother had to undo
every stitch and sew it again.

Cheap – the way the word came back to me when I was
at the party where I had chosen to wear the wrong kind
of clothes, as though some sense of style, of what is right
to wear, is bred into others but left out in me, like the time
I went to the faculty party

at Young Pie's house in suburban KC,
and everyone else was wearing short dresses and jeans
and I wore a floor length cocktail dress,

or the time I read my poems at the Ivy League College
and I chose a dress with big flowers on it when everyone else
was wearing tweed jackets and oxford cloth white shirts
and wool skirts that fell exactly below the knee
and neat little black or brown low heeled pumps and leather

bags I felt cheap and like I'd never learn to be anything else,
all those old cheap clothes still hanging on me,
like another skin, only this one I'd never
shed no matter how long I lived.

So Many Secrets

I've told in my poems secrets
I could never have told to anyone else,
Not face to face, not in person,
Writing things down is always easier,

Though sometimes it's taken me years to say it,
Years to write about something that I did
Or said or didn't do even thirty years ago,

Until I write it down and it loses some of its power
To sting, that bee sting of memory that burns
And burns, only words able to take away
The ache like baking soda and water
And in the end the poem to read
Until the memory of that shameful moment
Of cowardice or guilt is eased,

And we can go forward into our lives,
Leaving that memory behind.
We think of looking at the beautiful faces
Of these young people, the incredible faces,
The girl in the previous session who read her poem
And cried and cried. I know that moment
When we reach the cave
Full of grief and shame and love
From which all poems emerge.

What memory do I have
Of a secret I haven't shared
With anyone, not this white paper

With its neat blue lines,
Not this pen. Then I remember my father

Fired again from another job, and my mother's rage
At him, and of me standing in the doorway
Between them, my mother berating him
For not staying at his previous job,
For listening to his friend
That this new job would be a better one
And it turned out not to be,

So he had to crawl back to his old boss
And ask for his job back and his boss gave it
Back but not before he made him suffer,
Took away all his benefits, erased
Eight years on the job
With one flick of his pen

And my father, at ninety-one,
remembering that day,
His hands and voice shaking.
I remember how angry I was at him
For never having enough money,
For always choosing the wrong thing,
And how ashamed I am now
In his hot little parlor,
His torn plaid blanket
Covering his legs,
His eyes filled with the milky film
Of cataracts, and mine filled with tears.

Winter Dusk

The scythe of winter dusk cuts through the last of the sun
in the courtyard, the trees stripped of all leaves, their bark

black as coal. I remember the coal in the cellar in the house,
the huge coal furnace, the scraping of the shovel

on the cement floor, the marks when the coal was fed
through the furnace's hungry mouth. It was always dark

down in that cellar with its single light bulb hanging on an
electrical cord from a beam and its white-washed walls.

In back of the cellar, way past the furnace, was a wooden
room made of rough planks where my father's wine barrels

were kept and the wine press he used to make the wine from
the huge purple grapes he bought at the Farmer's Market

in Paterson. Leading down to the cellar was an uneven set
of rough cement steps that hugged the backside of the house.

Next to the house, the cracked driveway with the strip
of scraggly grass growing up the middle and the cement

of that driveway crumbling. Is it February that I think
of first in that house, February when even the little

city sun that sifted between the close set houses and the
factories wasn't strong enough to penetrate the bleakness?

Was it really the weather or this time of year? Was it
rather a part of living there, 19th Street, gray of neglect,

gray of lives going nowhere, gray of despair, gray of the fine
dust of crumbling cinder blocks, gray of sadness, gray

of the courtyard, with its patio and tree, and the window
of another professor with his lamp glowing in the darkening

night, gray of this courtyard miles removed from that
cement gray, old house gray, where I started out?

When I Was a Young Woman

When I was a young woman, I wore a white rubber girdle
though I only weighed 104 pounds and didn't have an ass

or at least I had a very flat one, but all the young women
I knew wore girdles with snaps attached to hold up

our nylon stockings. The girdle had little holes punched in it
to let it breathe, though actually it didn't breathe very well,

and it was difficult to get off. Now I wonder if that wasn't
the idea, underpants, white cotton, the girdle over them,

the stockings, a slip, a skirt, all those clothes intended
to protect our virginity which of course they never did.

It was a little like my mother's idea that if I was home
by 10 P.M. she had made sure I would remain a virgin,

or like the time, the third date I had with the man
I would later marry, when we pulled up in front of the house

in Dennis' old Plymouth and we sat talking, my back
against the door, while we discussed philosophy

because we thought we were great intellectuals.
My mother rushed out of the house in her robe,

her hair in pink foam curlers, a broom in her hand.
She used the handle to bang on the window and yelled,

"My daughter does not sit in front of the house in a car.
Get inside." Shy and awkward, Dennis leaped out

of the car to open the door for me. He barely said
goodbye before he jumped into the car to run away.

Of course, he did come back. I was so humiliated
I thought I'd never see him again, and of course,

the rubber girdle and the early curfew and all
the other efforts my mother made, didn't work at all.

The Cup

My fingers, raised and rounded, are a cup
holding a universe waiting to be filled
with stars, moon, dark November sky.
Outside the window, the night
is a black cape sprinkled with diamonds,
Inside this white room,
I write on yellow paper,
holding delicately in my mind
my life, fragile as a china cup,
so fine that my fingers show through
as pale blue shadows.

My Mother-in-Law

In the old photograph, my mother-in-law is still young and
slender in her fitted 1940s dress. She is holding Dennis

in her arms; he is six months old, wrapped in a blanket.
In the black and white photo I cannot tell what color

the blanket is, nor what color his hair is or his eyes,
but I can see that my mother-in-law has a firm body;

her hair is dark-colored and neat. She is almost beautiful
and since she is serious in the photo, her buck teeth

don't show. She is standing in the River Edge back yard,
their brand new house behind her. I sense that her life

is full of possibilities. She thinks she will bite into it
as easily as a peach. By the time of her first heart attack

when she is seventy-eight, she can't live alone anymore.
She has to move in with us, something she always vowed

she would never do. In the intervening years she has gained
one hundred pounds and lost it again; her wrinkled face sags

and her body, thin, is covered in loose flesh. After a couple
of years, Alzheimer's sets in. One night at 3 A.M,

I hear the front door slamming closed again and again.
I rush downstairs to find her sitting naked

on the couch, immensely pleased with herself. I hire
a Polish lady to take care of her, after she nearly sets fire

to the house. By the time she dies, seven years later,
she thinks people are coming out of the TV to get us.

She hits Dennis with her walker saying, "You're a bad son,
bad son, bad son!" She slams her rocker into the wall

so hard she makes a big hole in the plaster. Now when
I watch TV in the room I called her room, and look

at the picture of her when she was young, I cannot connect
that young woman with the hopeful face with the old,

raging woman I remember. When I see a picture of myself
at twenty-eight at my brother's wedding, a girl I nearly

don't recognize and look at myself now, I think
how we are all broken in half like this, a jagged line

like the pieces of a puzzle that just won't fit,
our image today in the mirror too much to bear.

Nail Clippings

On my desk, I saw a clipping from a nail. Is it mine?
I'm embarrassed that the person sitting across from me

will think it is mine. I can't keep my eyes off it,
the way I couldn't keep my eyes off the nose ring

that one of my workshop students at St. Mary's Festival
was wearing, when she came to me for her one-on-one

meetings about her work. She had beautiful dark hair
and lovely huge black eyes, but I couldn't stop

looking at that nose ring, couldn't stop wondering
how she was able to blow her nose. So now, sitting

at my new pale gray desk, the nail paring draws me
to it. I've heard of people who stole nail clippings

or hair from a person. I've heard that they're used
in voodoo or black magic to put the whammy

on someone. Maybe that's why all those Victorians
had that morbid fascination with death. Necklaces

with pendants containing hair of the dead,
or that picture I gave to Barbara that I found

in Antonina's shop, a picture of a beautiful
young woman in a high necked Victorian dress,

her shiny hair piled Gibson girl style high on her head,
but if I moved the picture a certain way, the face turned

into a death's head, and her body, a skeleton. I gave it
to Barbara as part of a birthday present because I thought

she'd be interested in it. I didn't realize until she opened it
that she might take it as an indication of her own mortality.

How stupid I am not to have realized how she'd feel
When I see her face, I realize that she thinks I did it on

purpose, instead of out of stupidity. I remember a story
I heard once about a woman who saved her bodily refuse

in shoeboxes in her closet. I always had this image
of those boxes stacked up on the shelf in a closet.

Imagine someone's surprise when they open
one of those boxes? Someone told me this story

before I got married. On our honeymoon I was nervous
around my husband whom I didn't know very well,

though I loved him, or the person I thought he was.
I went into the bathroom to take a shower. I stepped

into the shower and, when my new husband walked in,
I screamed. "You scared me." It was a long time

before he came into the bathroom with me.
How careful we are of our bodies, fearing loss and afraid

of giving things away. We guard our hearts the same way.
My mother always said, "The more I gave away, the more

I had to give." I try to live like that. I don't want to be one
of those people who are so afraid of losing something,

they store themselves in shoe boxes so that, when they decide to give something of themselves away,

they find only dried up and desiccated lumps, and not the treasure they first stored so carefully away.

Poem to John

You call me more often now,
ask me to come down to visit
and sound as though you mean it.
I used to feel you didn't know what to say to me
and it made me so sad. The long silence
that I'd try to fill with chattering words scattered
in the air, meaningless as ticker tape,
I'd say something and you'd sigh
and answer me, your voice heavy with resistance,
and I'd hang up the phone and cry
because you, whose hand I held as we crossed the street,
you on whose bed I sat until you fell asleep,
you who used to talk to me, closed up against me
as though I were your enemy, and you begrudged every
    reluctant word.

Now you call me and I feel that you have something you need
to say, though you don't quite get to it.
Maybe it helps to hear my voice as it helps me to hear yours,
Maybe you are starting to know that your children,
who cling to you now that they are small,
will move away from you.
You, too, will be the person on the other end of the line
while your children leave those huge pauses in the empty air,
your children, who breathe when you breathe,
who fall asleep in your arms,
who trust you above all others,
one day your children will be lost to you.

II

I sigh when the phone rings. When I pick it up out of its tan cradle, it is your voice I hear, deep-timbered and heavy with grief. "What is it, John?" I ask, as though you would actually tell me what it is that drags your voice down and fills it with sorrow. "I'm just tired, Ma," you say. I remember you as a little boy, bent over your model tanks and figures, your tongue clasped between your teeth, your whole body concentrating on painting the miniature faces on the figure that will sit in the seat of this tank. Every knife in the house burned from being held to the flame so you could cut and shape the models. You were always self-contained. Spent hours in your room with the heat turned up high, your books piled around your bed, track shoes, and shirts heaped in a corner. I should have known then how you would move away from me, how necessary is this severing and reshaping of our lives. The burned knife of distance changes what we are, mother and son, a phone wire the only tentative cord left between us. Words that offer comfort stuck like a fishbone in my throat. I would give anything to erase the sorrow from your voice. I say: "Take Care. Are you taking your vitamins? Are you eating?"

III

I remember when I sat on your bed
And we'd talk, how you needed
To have me there.

A huge distance opens between us,
Not only of highway and town,
But like the bowl formed by the Catskills
In which fog and mist drift
So that everything that has grown familiar
Is suddenly altered.
I thought I would always know you,
Recognize you anywhere no matter
How much time had passed,
But all my certainties disintegrate
As we struggle to find the ease
We once had with each other,
The words that floated between us,
Free as balloons.

You answer my questions
With yes or no, your secrets hidden
In the heavy timbre of your voice,
A grief I hear running like a cord
Through everything you say,

And I, who would do anything
To make you happy, am helpless
Before your silence, cannot find you
Through this fog that ripples
Between us, the way you recede from me
Until I am afraid a day will come
When I won't remember your face
Or the feel of your high cheekbones
Under my hand.

Window

In my third floor room
I am floating
above
this small city
lost
beneath outer vastness.
The endless mountains
are dark charcoal smudges
against the gray sky,

and trees, bare
of leaves, sweep
the clouds like brooms.

Rainbow Over the Blue
Ridge Mountains

All day the rain has been rattling its tin shield
against the roof, but now, the noise stilled,
I look out the window and am surprised
by a rainbow over the Blue Ridge Mountains,
in the distance. A huge arc of pink and yellow
and green, amazing and exquisite.

How rushed my life has been,
how fortunate to have this week
to return to the natural world again
and to listen to the first bird
chirping after rain.

Return

I ride Route 17 West, and the mountains lift
And circle the road, mountains in front of me
And the curve of others to the right and left,

The evergreens' dark feathers brush the sky,
And the trees on the hills, bereft of leaves,
Stand stiff and straight as pencil strokes,
Close together and pointing skyward,

So perfect and symmetrical the lines
They could be an artist's rendition
Of winter mountains.

I try to make a picture of them
In my mind, black pencil strokes
Separated by white snow.

Song in Praise of Spring

I fill the round blue bowl
of morning with silence
broken only
by the soft silver speech of birds
in the dogwood's bare branches.
Under the radiant veil
of this spring sky.
I imagine
the stars shining.

Elvis Presley Is Alive and Well on Lincoln Avenue in Fair Lawn, New Jersey

I am driving down Lincoln Avenue in my little red Honda when I see Elvis Presley at the window of a boxy two family house, with two porches stacked one on top of the other. In the window that looks out on the first floor porch, Elvis Presley sits, his face in profile. There is a light behind him. Even as evening falls in on us, he is clearly outlined. The next time I pass that house, I look for him. This time, in addition to the Elvis in the window, there's a big plaster record and another Elvis, sitting in a chair on the porch. Each day when I pass the house, there's a new addition until the porch has a sitting Elvis, a plastic guitar, a cardboard cutout of a pink Cadillac, a standing Elvis, and an Elvis, knees bent, pelvis thrust out in that Elvis stance, that way of pushing out his hips that shocked America and made teenagers love him. One day when I pass the house, everything is gone save one torn shade: no Elvis at the window, no sitting Elvis on the porch, no pink Cadillac, no record, no standing Elvis, no Elvis in his pelvic rock.

Where did they go to, these people so caught in another era, they who spent this much thought on building a shrine to Elvis, that fire that burned and flared across the American sky forty years ago? Each place they move, imagine them carting all the fake Elvis dummies and cardboard cutouts, filling their lives with Elvis, raising Elvis from the dead, pulling on his skin, driving all the girls to a frenzy with their songs.

The Herald News Calls Paterson
a "Gritty City"

When I leave Passaic County Community College at dusk,
the sky is the most amazing color – deep violet and luminous,
like an old woman who is smiling suddenly looks young.
The courthouse dome is outlined against the sky,
the rococo arches of the old post office,
the clock tower of the new federal building,
starkly simple, and the clock tower of city hall,
ornate and elegant.

I love the voice of this city, the eyes
of its people, the whooshing sound of the Great Falls,
the old mill that has become a museum,
its brick work shining in sunlight.

I see the old men sleeping in the dumpster,
the prostitute resting against the walls of St. Paul's
Church, the empty crack vials
in the gutter, the transvestites on the corner,
but, under the gritty surface, a fresh energy rises,
and it is the heart of the city –
it beats in the shiny copper of the fountain
in Cianci Street park, in the old men in the Roma Club,
shrewd and wary, squinting against cigarette smoke,
playing Italian card games and drinking espresso.

It beats in the chests of the new immigrants –
Iranians and Colombians, Cubans and Syrians
Dominicans and Indians, carting their hopes to this city
and dreaming, and in the young men with the gangsta pants,
their underwear showing, and in the bravado
of the girl with the braids and the yellow barrettes
and her starched dress and in the little boy

with his torn sneakers and his jean jacket
and the handsome clean lines of his face.
I sing this song for them, for all of them,
the saved and the lost, the ones who will survive
and the ones who will not. I sing for the Jamaican family
and their new restaurant and their hard work
and the young Cuban woman who wants to make money
from her poetry, and for those who will find
the city's heart beating under grit
and who will hear its music
and sing along.

The Great Escape

The recruiters for the army/navy/air force
sit behind plain wooden tables.
covered with leaflets on the service,
an officer pictured, bright-eyed and clean,
all his brass buttons shining.

The recruiters, white and clean-shaven,
their close-cropped light hair,
their eyes blue as marbles, stand out in this lobby
at Passaic County College in Paterson, New Jersey,
filled with young black/brown skin and voices in ghetto slang,
and Puerto Rican women in elastic, day-glo pants,
and slender Latino men with clipped moustaches,
and dapper smiles. Out of the crowd of moving,
circulating students, first Juan Garcia, then Kevin Clark,
drifts over to the recruiters.

I hear the sales pitch on how the service gives you a chance
to learn a trade and to have a career, and when you get out,
they even give you a scholarship to college.
Kevin's face turns hopeful, the path
to a better life opening in his mind like a highway
out of this city and the only life he's known,
and Juan listens and he, too, believes.

They drift back to the group. Others replace them.
All day the recruiters talk and talk till finally
at nightfall Jose Jemenez and Khemi Freeman
and George McKay and Keisha Lynette return
to the tables, sign their names to long, complicated forms
that they don't comprehend, the path out of the city
smooth as greased metal.

After Broadway,
after the Alexander Hamilton Welfare Hotel,
after the graffiti on the walls,
after the pimp strutting his four women,
after the garbage in the gutters,
after the screaming woman,
this offer, the brass buttons
on the suit of the army lieutenant,
his polished shoes, and the Air Force
corporal, sharp in her blue uniform and neat,
shining hair, seem to hold out golden keys

to José Jemenez, Khemi Freeman,
George McKay, Keisha Lynette,
that they hope will set them free.

On TV ten days after the outbreak
of the war, the cameraman
takes a picture of some young people
waiting in Saudi Arabia for the fighting
to begin. The camera scans
the untried, untouched faces of the soldiers.
"We've been waiting so long,"
Mason Brown says, "I just want it
to start," meaning the fighting,
the tanks massing at the border,
the ground troops waiting.
"This is where I want to be," he says.

Noise

The noisiest place I remember is the Passaic County Jail where they took our Leadership Paterson group on a tour, pushing us ahead in front of the women and children waiting to see their husbands or boyfriends. They let them go inside one at a time, so even when I pass the jail at midnight, women and children are waiting in winter cold and summer heat. We were herded inside. The sheriff was proud of his jail, which was built to house 1200 prisoners but holds 2800. Cells for two hold six prisoners, two sleeping under the bottom bunk on a mat on the floor. He is proud of the fact that the state pays him forty-eight dollars a day to feed prisoners and he only spends twenty-four dollars. He does not return the rest; instead, he operates the jail at a profit. Its inmates are mostly Hispanic and Black. They are squeezed into day rooms too small for that many men. The noise level is so high it feels as if my ear drums will burst: men shouting, playing cards, the TV blaring, radios playing. The hot smell of too many bodies mingles with the noise. I imagine a circle of hell exactly like this place and I wonder how they keep from going mad. I want to get out, to get away from the crew cut and the blue eyes of the sheriff, his self-satisfied smile, and the horrible concert of sound that follows us out of the jail and all the way home.

What I Do Is

Leave dishes in the sink

Look my name up in the Internet and feel happy
Because there are ninety-nine references to me
In one search engine alone

Sleep a lot

Sit on the couch and go through a pile of papers
That never seems to get smaller

Go to the post office and the bank

Collect the mail

Do two minutes worth of anemic exercise

Hear Dennis's shuffling feet in the kitchen

Look through more papers, which I'm sure
Are multiplying like some wild virus
Look at my treadmill, which sits, unused
And stares accusingly at me

Listen to the teapot's whistle

Talk to my daughter on the phone

Stop myself from calling my son
Since I'm afraid of annoying my daughter-in-law

Go to the red, white, and blue thrift shop
To pretend I'm exercising

Give advice to my children and friends, advice
They didn't ask for and don't want

Screen my phone calls

Stall calling people I should call but don't want to

Have dreams in which all the people who are long since
Dead speak to me.

Breathing

When you were still full of the work that filled
your day and evening, when you couldn't sit idle,

even after the evening meal was cooked and the dishes
washed and the kitchen cleaned, after the final chores

of the day were finished, you'd sit in the brown chair
in your little parlor, Dad in his recliner next to you,

the television on, and you, crocheting at amazing
speed, turning out so many afghans that all the children

and the grandchildren have two or three apiece. When
we went to the big bin behind the Bunker Hill rug factory

to pick out the discarded rolls of yarn, you were happy
to have so much yarn, free for the taking. You told me then

that your mother always visited you in the night to bring
you news, and you promised you'd visit me too. I wonder now

that you are eight years dead, now that they boxed you up
in the mausoleum drawer where I never visit you

because I cannot think of you closed in that steel cabinet,
closed away from the earth you loved. You sold your

cemetery plots because you were afraid we wouldn't take care
of your graves. I cannot think of you, who were always moving,

forced to lie in that one narrow space. I was with you
when you died. I saw your eyes turn opaque and knew

that you were gone, only your body left on that table.
I remember that you told me, when even my doctor

brother thought you were dead, that you saw your mother
and sisters and it was so beautiful there in that place

filled with flowers and light. I want to think that you aren't
stuck in that drawer at Holy Angels Cemetery, but instead

in that heaven of light, walking those paths with your mother
and sisters. I think of how your mother visited you

all those years after she died, and I have waited for you,
hoped to feel your weight at the edge of my bed, hoped

to see you standing in the doorway coming toward me yet,
when I hear your words in my mouth, I know you are with me.

Sometimes I Forget That You're Dead

Papa, sometimes I forget that you're dead.
I start to drive toward your house, and remember.

You've been gone now nearly a year.
Your house emptied by strangers

who went through your closets and sold off
the bits and pieces of your life.

After visiting you every day for nine years,
I could not bear to go into your house

and clean it out, so I hired a couple to hold
an estate sale. When the sale was over,

your house denuded, only a few torn scraps
of paper and knick-knacks were left.

Old material and magazines were tossed
in tangled and dusty lumps.

I thought about how Mom would have hated
the shame of this neglect,

she worked so many years to keep the house spotless.
Before you died, you wanted your life to be over,

caught as you were in a world bounded by your bed
and wheelchair, all your friends long since dead,

only me to visit you each day. At the end
you stopped speaking, even lost interest in politics,

sighed away the heaviness of your days. Your eyes
no longer lit up when you saw me, and then,

you were gone. You decided enough,
you turned over and stopped breathing.

I forget you are dead, your house emptied
and sold. I tucked a deck of cards in your coffin

because I know how you'd missed the endless card games
you played with your friends. They were glad

to see you. Papa, I hope that you are sitting
under some grape arbor, your friends

around you, every day a perfect fall day,
the sun warm as my hand on your face,

I who am here, thinking of you.

This Leaf

On this country road I see the leaf, and its wide hand, its splayed fingers seem to reach out to me. I feel compelled to pick it up and carry it with me. It is maple syrup brown, with a center stem that ends in a foot with three separate toes like the foot of a chicken, at least, I think chickens have three toes, although my knowledge of country life is extremely limited. I haven't seen a chicken's foot in more than forty years. I do remember going to the chicken man on River Street with my mother, rows of caged chickens, squeaking and squawking, the floor covered with sawdust and chicken feathers, the smell of fresh blood, my mother and all the other Italian ladies buying their fresh chickens and I stood with my mother while she picked out the bird she wanted, and the chicken man plucked it out of its cage and went into the back and wrung its neck or chopped off its head or both, I'm not sure. I was so young. There was a lot I missed. What I do remember is the noise and bustle of the place, the way the women's faces looked as they chattered with each other, my mother, going about the serious business of life, was self-contained, her feelings carefully hidden behind her eyes, her face brown as the underside of this leaf, its lines and tributaries, a complex map to a country she preferred to keep to herself, fearing the scissored tongues of the Riverside gossips. When I turn the leaf over, the sunshine on it lights it up, the way mother's face lit up once we were back in the 17th Street apartment, and she looked at me for a moment, before she started bustling around that kitchen, preparing the chicken to be cooked by burning off the feathers on the stove. Practical and no nonsense, my mother loved us fiercely, protectively, but she could be tough and strong. She taught us by what she did; to rely on each other and the family. "Friends," she said, "eh, friends, they only stay around when things are good." Maybe that's why this leaf reminds me of her; the way she was when she was dying, like this leaf, perky and on the ground, even though it's January and should have crumbled to pieces months ago.

I Don't Know

I don't know what it is I want or how
I managed to make this room look

Like it had been in a tornado, blankets,
Pillows, books, papers, bags full of junk,

My decrepit couch – all the rubble of my life
Scattered and messy. My mother is in the room

With me, though she's been dead for ten years.
She's telling me what a slob I am, and why

Can't I learn to be neat and to put things away?
I don't know why in two minutes I can take

A neat room, and even when I'm trying to be careful,
I can turn it into a disaster. I don't know how

To change myself into the daughter my mother wanted,
More like my own perfect daughter who cleaned out

My entire garage, filled to the brim with paper and books
And trash, so that now it looks better than my entire house,

My beautiful daughter who worked hard and lifted
So many heavy boxes until one box was too much,

A box, "not even that big," she says, and she heard something
Snap. She had to sit down, then, in such pain that tears were

Running down her face when I found her. She hasn't been
Able to move without pain since then, despite the Tylox

My brother prescribes which should knock out any pain,
But doesn't seem to touch this one. I don't know why

It seems to have skipped a generation – the way my daughter
Is willing to work for hours at a stretch without stopping,

The way she thinks she can do anything, just like my mother
Who would come into my house, waving her arms wildly

Over her head, and shout, "What did I do wrong?
What did I do wrong? Look at this mess!"

She'd start cleaning up and cursing all the things
I didn't know how to do, muttering to herself

While she cleaned furiously. One day
when I told her to get out, because she was

Annoying me, she said I could live the way I wanted,
But she'd never come back. Today, watching my daughter

Who carries my mother's efficient genes, my daughter
I always depend on more than any mother should,

I would call my mother back from the dead, ask her to help
Me clean up the mess. I can almost see her sturdy body,

Moving like a dervish through my rooms till they are clean
And neat. I promise, if she'd only come back, this time

To say thank you, and try to explain
How much I didn't know, and the way now,

Even after all this time, I still need her.

The Story of My Day

I get up at 6 A.M., drive all the way to Trenton
for a meeting where I am held captive for five hours

in a crowded room, drive two hours back to my house
and get right back into the car, after picking up

my books and poems, drive down Route 4
over the George Washington Bridge onto

the Westside Highway and down to 12th Street
and zigzag toward the eastside, squeezing past

parked trucks and screeching cabs and, finally,
head toward the lower east side where I arrive

by 5 P.M. though my reading is not until 7.
The neighborhood is seedy and rundown.

Across the street a huge project sits bleak
and hopeless. I'm afraid to get out of my car,

fearing it will be stolen. I park my car and wait
until it is legal to park at the meter. I drop in four

quarters for an hour and go into the Bodega
where I buy my dinner, a bottle of water

and a bag of barbecued potato chips, and where
the man behind the counter calls me *mami*

and is nice to me as he argues with one
of his customers who refuses to pay for a bag

of chips, saying they were free. By the time I get
back to the car, only fifteen minutes have passed,

so I read over my poems and munch on the potato
chips and drink the water, though the potato chips

leave my face and lips and teeth orange, and I use
a Purell Sanitizing Hand towel that my daughter bought

for me to keep in my car, and I try to clean up my face
and teeth, hoping that I got it all and that people

in the store haven't spotted me scarfing down
potato chips. It is still too early to go inside,

and this is the way I spend my day.

In My Family

In my family we're all tenacious, decide what we want and go after it.

We work hard, moving forward, when we're exhausted, and think we can't move one inch more. I wonder if it's in the genes, this need to finish everything we start, this belief that hard work and perseverance will get us through. My sister kept going to work for months after she had seizures and couldn't walk. Her live-in aide took her to work in a wheelchair, pushing her down the road, because the sidewalks in Hawthorne aren't handicapped accessible.

My father had a degenerative disease of the spine. He dragged one paralyzed leg behind him wherever he went, and went he did, driving until he was eighty-seven years old, cloth around the pedals of the car so he could reach the brake, one shoe built up to compensate for the unevenness of his legs, driving to his friends' houses to play cards and visit, driving to the courthouse in Paterson to file a petition for his friends or register the legal papers he drew up, his body failing him, but his mind sharp and willing him on.

My son John wants to think he is not like us. I hear how even at thirty-two he takes responsibility for his life, how he gets up at 5 A.M., so he can be at his office by 5:30, how he handles the complex legal problems of a large corporation, working straight through till he returns at 6 P.M. to help with the children and to deal with the house, the yard, repairs. He takes everything seriously. I love the way John carries his son in his arms, the child running to him for comfort and the way they speak to each other without words. I know that even my son, who wants to think he is not like our family, is driven as we are, to keep on going, no matter what.

These are the things my mother taught us by example, my mother who tripped over our skates when we were children and got up and walked the twelve blocks to Ferraro Coat Factory on River Street. She worked until noon, walked back home to make our lunches, and then walked back to work. Only after she came home at 3:30, so she could be there when we got home from school, did she collapse into a chair unable to move. When she came back from the hospital clinic with a cast on her leg, fourteen bones in her foot broken, she had to rest her leg on a stool. That was one of the few times in her life that I saw her cry, not because of the pain, but because she couldn't do the work she told herself she had to do.

Doris Day

Your movies always ended with marriage,
promising life lived happily ever after.
Rock Hudson was always your groom,
the handsome man who chased you
through numerous misunderstandings
until you agreed to be his forever.
In The Rivoli or The Fabian Theater,

we watched you, longed
with all our sixteen year old hearts
for your life: the luxurious white
peignoir, the roses on the breakfast tray,
the absence of any real tragedy,
a world without dead children

or atrophied love, your life lived
on the surface where everything
you ever wanted was finally yours.
We followed you adoringly down
that red-carpeted aisle, the white
wedding gown, the tiered wedding cake,

the limousine, the handsome groom,
and were shocked, then, to find
it was only a dream after all,
a celluloid fantasy we wanted to live out.
We tried for years not to know
That love often led to grief and sorrow,

that a house can be empty even
when it is full of people, that loss
is a burden we must carry alone.
Oh perky Doris, even you must

have suspected that what you
were selling was counterfeit.
Where are you now, Doris Day?
Were you as fooled as we were
by those Technicolor moments,
some part of you wanting to believe
that your life, too, could be easy
and smooth, all scented cream
and satin, and that like Sleeping Beauty

you needed a man to wake you?
Are you longing now for sleep
into which you can escape
the monotony of marriage
lived in black and white?

Nancy Drew, I Love You

Nancy Drew, at eleven, I loved you, read every one
of your books, over and over. You became
the best friend I didn't have that year.

I imagined following you into caves and woods,
climbing rope ladders, exploring secret passages
in old mansions. In my mind, your flashlight, large

as a whale's eye, illuminated mysteries.
Stepping into that circle of light, I left behind
the skinny Italian girl, mute with shyness,
timid about roller skating on slippery slate
sidewalks, too afraid of water

to ever learn to swim, frightened
by the speed of bicycles and roller coasters,
afraid of teachers who looked at me
and found me lacking.

Gladly, I would have become you, pulled on
your white skin like a silk dress. I pretended
I could be you, outspoken and gregarious,
brave and wily. I imagined you would want me

to be your friend. I imagined
I could go into our dank immigrant cellar
with its coal stove and mouse traps

and its smell of fermenting grapes,
and behind the huge wine barrels,
I would find a secret room like the kind

you always found in your books. Nancy,
I wanted to be you, despite all the evidence
that nothing could transform me,

I, who stared at the rope in gym
as though it were alive, and struggled
to climb up one foot before I fell

to the polished floor. I knew you had
so many things I wanted: your best
friend, your middle class life, your big house,

a life of adventure and scrapes regarded
with mild disapproval and admiration
by your lawyer father, your fearlessness

in the face of danger, a fearlessness
that belonged nowhere in my Paterson world
where my Italian mother insisted we had to stay

on the cement front stoop. There she knew
we couldn't get into trouble. Through that long
summer, I sat on a wooden chair, my legs resting

on the porch railing, my mind transported
into your world as I followed you
up mountains and into caves. From my porch,

that safe harbor, I could have adventures
without ever having to endure
a sprained ankle or a scraped knee.

Nancy Drew, I still love you
for taking me with you,
carrying me away from the tight

confines of my life, to a place
where everything is possible
and bravery is common

and miraculous as stars.

Last Night My Mother Came Back

Last night my mother came back. I saw her
in the distance, her body draped in wisps of fog,

ethereal as she never was in life, my sturdy
mother, her feet always planted on the ground,

practical and no-nonsense and scolding.
Why doesn't she move toward me

instead of moving away? My sister tells me
my mother visited her in that North Carolina

hospital room, my mother, who never traveled,
who in her life had only been to Italy and New Jersey,

came to my sister. My father came too. My sister
woke up and they were there, sitting in straight-backed

chairs near her bed. They tell my sister to be careful;
then they talk about her children

and the family and what she can do to save herself.
"It was so nice to see them," my sister says. I am hurt

that they do not visit me. When she was dying,
my mother said she couldn't wait until I arrived

every day. My sister, who has always run away
from things she could not face, had to be forced

to visit, but I knew my mother needed me.
I had to be there with her, that swollen belly,

the cancer turning her skin as yellow as a legal pad,
her small hand soft in mine. Now I watch my mother

move away from me, watch her turn, one last time
to look at me, her smile almost a hand on my face,

her love, as always, delivered in gestures
rather than words. I mention her every day,

this woman who taught us to search for grace
in the center of our days.

Laura, Now That You Are Gone

Sometimes I start
To walk across the street,
To your house before I realize
You died more than a month ago.
The plaque you sent me
With its sentimental words
And pink flowers
Hangs in my den.
You must have known
You would die soon.
And wanted me to know
You loved me,
Though we didn't say it
To one another.

Sister, who was so different from me,
Sister, who called for me and I came to you,
Even slept all night in your hospital room
In a hard plastic chair to make sure
You didn't die in the night,
Sister, whose frail, twisted hand
I held in mine,
Sister, who called me on my birthday,
Though you were having trouble breathing,
"Mary, Mary, Where are you?"
And then you sang "Happy Birthday to you,
Happy Birthday to you."

All your energy and desire to live
Caught in your husky, faltering voice

That I hear in my head
When I think of you.

Since Laura Died

Alex, since Laura died, I hear the flat timbre
of your voice, the heaviness in it, the sorrow,

and know that some part of you refuses
to let her go. She held a corner of your world up

for you and without her, a blank space
you don't know how to fill.

Older sister to her baby brother, the roles
played themselves out even after we all grew up,

and you were the doctor and she, your nurse.
In your office she told you what to do,

as she did when we were children
And pretended she was our mother, and we

came to her for help with the American world
Mamma didn't understand. Now I call you,

though I know I can't fill the space where she was,
so many years the surrogate mother, the tie between

the two of you stronger than the one between us.
It was only after she moved to North Carolina

so her daughter could take care of her,
that I realized that you called her every day,

that you paid her $400 a month over her pension,
that just hearing her voice made you feel safe,

and now, with Laura gone and Mom and Dad gone, too,
who will hold the screen between us and

the empty valley where they all vanished, leaving us
alone and trembling in our suburban houses where we don't

know the neighbors and my voice on the phone
isn't enough to comfort you?

The Studebaker Silver Hawk

Dennis talks about the Studebaker Silver Hawk his father
bought when he was a teenager, a very cool car for a middle-
   aged man,
light blue and silver. When Dennis shows a picture of it
to his boyhood friend, their eyes light up. Dick says,
"Your father let you drive that car. My father never let me
drive his car. He told me to go out to work to earn the money

to buy my own car." In the old album, the car is parked
in the driveway of the white colonial in River Edge.
It gleams with its sharp edges and polished chrome.
I dated Dick first and met Dennis at Dick's house.
I stopped seeing anyone in the room once Dennis
came in and took out his guitar and sang.

By the time I met Dennis, the Silver Hawk
was only a shining memory, a light in Dennis' eyes
when he talks about it, even now, thirty years later.
When I met him, he was driving a black Pontiac
with dark brown tweed upholstery torn in spots
and a narrow windshield and side windows

with little flaps that opened so you could drive along
and feel the wind on your face. We parked on the Palisades
and looked at the lights of New York across the Hudson,
before we necked and petted and French kissed, until we both
were in a frenzy of unfulfilled lust. He drove me home
with his arm around me. I sat as close to him as I could.

This was the early 1960s and nice Catholic girls did not
go all the way; though my Italian blood was not into
denial of the flesh. If he had asked me,
I would have resisted and then given in
But as a nice Catholic boy, he respected me.
I couldn't break out of the cast of rules that kept me

acting the way I thought I should, afraid of getting pregnant,
of having a policeman shine his light on us, on my
unbuttoned blouse, my unsnapped bra, the heat in my body,
the steamed up windows of his car, the other cars lined up
in a row on that dark lookout.
On our wedding day, my father rented a limousine for us.
After we were married, the photographer asked us to look out

the back window of the limo so he could take our picture.
It is that picture I think of first when I think of us,
that girl and boy, so young and unknowing, looking
toward a future they have no way of imagining,
just as I look at the young woman walking toward me,
who has taken her child to the bus and who reminds me

of myself at her age. Perhaps it is the spring in her step
that makes me remember mornings when in half light
we made love before I got dressed to walk the children
to school, my happiness in the way I walked
and the half smile I never could erase from my face.
Today seeing her and remembering, I realize

this is what Dennis and Dick feel when they speak
of the Silver Hawk and the shining they recapture
for a moment before it too vanishes like all time
that passes through our fingers elusive as fog.

Signposts

Today I found an old album with pictures of us,
from 1977, taken on our first trip to Italy.

It is our first trip without our children.
The camera captures us sitting together

at a table with other couples; lifted toward you,
my face so alive and glowing, I might

even be beautiful. I remember finding that I was shy
as I had been as a young girl with all these

strangers who seem foreign to me with their
interest in spending as much money as possible

at each stop of the tour bus. We are not
like them. We feel awkward when they get on the bus

showing off rings, watches, handbags, shoes,
coral pins. We tend to draw together

feeling our difference. We walk. You hold my
hand and our shoulders touch. "Look at the love birds,"

someone says. How right we are for each other, traveling
together in this country of my ancestors, miles

from the mountains where my parents were born, and
as the tour moves toward southern Italy, I start to see faces

that seem familiar, places that look like the places
my mother described when she talked about San Mauro.

The farther south we travel, the more at home I feel,
the dialect familiar and clear. I look back across

all the years between then and now, and see us: you, in your
glasses with heavy black frames, and my face

that couldn't possibly look so untouched, but does.
Pictures, memories. You stand in front of Bernini's

horses in Rome, I, at Pompeii, both of us in a Venetian
gondola where I almost fell into the filthy water

of the Canal. Signposts in our lives. Innocence
palpable, lives yet to move through so much loss.

Geography of Scars

An art that heals and protects itself is a geography of scars.
Wendell Berry

And though I have loved you for more than half my life,
Though we have grown into each other's arms
So that when I am away from you,
I imagine you are with me, our lives,
Gnarled and pitted as the bark of our oak trees,
This illness has moved in with us, a dark presence,
A shadow that hovers behind us as we walk
The path of our days.

I sit in our den with a book in my hands
And hear you call me,
Know by the tone of panic in your voice
That something is wrong.
I find you stuck to the floor,
Help me, you say, and I try.
I push you from behind, touch your foot,
Hold a ruler out in front of you, all the things
That are supposed to help you to move, but don't.

I bring you another pill and then we wait
Until the medicine starts to work
And you are able to walk a few feet to a chair.

I would moan and cry if only it would not hurt you.
Instead I retreat into my book again,
Try not to see the map of our future,
Knowing its lines and angles lead to a place
Where I will trace the geography of my grief,
These scars that remain when you,
Whom I have loved for so long, are gone.

In the New Millennium

In the new millennium, I still will be sitting behind my desk
in the chaos of my office, papers spilling from uneven stacks
around me, sirens sounding outside my windows. The phones
ring so often that a friend I hired to help me tells me
before he quits that the office is like being caught
in the bowels of the Titanic when it is sinking.

In the new millennium I still will be rushing off to poetry
readings and workshops, driving to airports
and down highways.

In the new millennium, you will be waiting for me
when I get home, though last night was the worst night yet,
you unable to move for hours, even the increased medicine
not working, and the new millennium rushing toward us,
only a few weeks left, and maybe then,
when the ball drops in Times Square, maybe it
will bring the magic pill that will cure you so you will be able
to move without help.

In the new millennium, I won't be able to lose any
weight and, at a meeting when I know I shouldn't, I will
stand up and speak out for what I know is right and people
in the room will stare and even my friends will avert their eyes,
though afterwards they will say, "Oh, you have so much
courage. I agreed with you, but I couldn't say it."

In the new millennium I will be exuberantly happy
when I hear my daughter's voice on the phone or when she
rushes down to New Jersey from Boston to see me and I will
lean on her more than I should.

In the new millennium I will be unable to find the
right words to reach my son, our conversations like pushing a
boulder up a mountain.

In the new millennium, Paterson streets will be littered
with the lives of the broken and forgotten, the shuffling men
with wild eyes and the lady in the wheelchair
who rides down the center of the street
in noon-hour traffic and curses anyone
who attempts to help her, even the policeman
whom she hits with her chair.

And in the new millennium, politics will be corrupt and big
money will buy votes, the gap between the rich and the poor
will grow wider, and the rivers more polluted.
In the new millennium, I will see the cup of the world
as half full rather than half empty, beauty even
in the polluted sky, the child reaching up to her mother
in front of city hall and the mother's arms gathering
the child up, her face softening,
her cheek against her child's hair.

When I Leave You

When I leave you in the kitchen doorway, drive
out of the garage with you watching, I realize
how your face grows more and more vulnerable,
worry lines etched in your skin.

Before I left, you said, "Don't worry about me.
I'll be all right. I won't be lonely. Call me
every night," but I don't know how
you will manage.

If I could I would find that old photo of you,
the one of you standing at the dock
in Martha's Vineyard, the white boats
bobbing behind you, John's hand in yours.
John is about two years old; he is wearing
a turquoise sweatshirt and blue jeans,
and you are wearing khaki pants
and a blue windbreaker.

Your face, in its horn-rimmed spectacles,
looks so young, your skin,
clear and glowing, your crewcut
catching and holding the light.
You look strong and healthy,
your shoulders wide inside
the windbreaker, your body, tall
and unbent. I wish I could
superimpose that photo
of your young, healthy self
over the person I am holding now

in my arms who is disappearing.
I would cut you out of that
picture like a paper doll, leave
little flaps to attach to you.
I could pretend that our lives
will go on as we thought they would
that day in Martha's Vineyard
when the world was singing to us
and everything ahead of us
was filled with light...

Grief

Grief is a long hallway, a door
That slams shut in the dark
Grief is the hand clamped
On my throat when I watch you
Struggle to move or when I hear
Your feet dragging and tripping
On the kitchen linoleum

The sound of your feet trying
To dislodge themselves
From the places where they
Are inexplicably stuck
The horrible staccato
Of your struggle

I pretend to be deaf
And blind, pretend that you are
The same as you were ten years ago
Five, even one, knowing
We will not go to the theater

Together in our old age
As I thought we would
Or travel together
Knowing that as March vanishes
And April opens its glorious hands
I travel the long road of grief
toward you, my loneliness

Each day deepens, as you move
Away from me, and I
Watch you go, my helpless
Hands hanging at my sides
My mouth calling your name.

These Are Words I Have Said

These are words I have said, over and over.
I count them as if they were carved beads
on the rosary my mother fingered each night,
but my prayers are not strong enough
to stop the hunger
of the disease that each day devours
more of what you once were.

Even your ankles are pitiful,
all bone and stretched flesh,
and your eyes have the stunned look
of birds who have smashed into a window.

Love, I would give you the warmth
of my body, the energy that surges
through me, if only I could.
In my arms now you seem insubstantial.

I am holding on to you as hard
as I can. I refuse to let you go:
is that the prayer I've been searching for,
the one that will save you?

Poem to My Husband
of Thirty-Three Years

Love, I wish I could be angry with you for leaving
when I need you here. You aren't even
leaving all at once: instead you seem
to grow smaller, thinner with each day,

your eyes baffled. You take up less and less space;
I want to hate you for the way you're disappearing.
I have trouble hearing your muted voice
and have to ask you to repeat yourself.

Your walk is so silent, I am often startled
to find you behind me, as though you are
becoming a ghost, parts of you pared away.
Even the air doesn't move when you move.

Sometimes when I come into the house, I call
and call, the house so still I am sure no one is in it,
until you rise up out of your basement room,
after what seems like a long time of shouting

your name, and I grumble, "It's like living
with a dead person." The past, iridescent
and elusive, floats away from us.
I drag the present with me
like a heavy suitcase wherever I go.

Traveler's Advisory

Because there is nowhere to go
Because distance tears
Because I have lived in a big old house
Because I like my little apartment
Because I telephone my husband every night
Because I look out my windows at the lights of Binghamton
Because I can read until late at night without bothering anyone
Because there is something delicious about loneliness
Because loneliness is a choice
Because the third day of each week I feel your need
pulling at me over telephone wires and I say
I'll be home tomorrow and I feel guilty for enjoying
these few months in my own place, suddenly set down
in this new territory without ties:
no husband, children, grandchildren, friends,
only a few people know my phone number
Because the silence of my place is blessed
Because the mountains outside the city are smudges
of charcoal against the gray sky
Because by the fourth day without you the loneliness
is greater than my need to be alone
Because on Route 17 barreling toward you in my Honda,
listening to poetry on my car tape player and watching
the road unwinding before me, the evergreens blur
Because, finally, I make the last quick turn
into my driveway and you are waiting.

Water Chestnut

The water chestnut is so perfectly formed,
like a fossil or a flower caught in dark metal,
the tip of it perfect, such attention to detail, grace,

it could be a forsythia leaf carved out of stone
or a bird perhaps, a winged thing. When I turn it
over in my hand, I see that it could be the head

of a steer or a goat. How its forms lend themselves
to conjecture, how impossible to capture as one thing
or another, the way we all are hidden under our skins,

the person on the outside, one thing, and the person
within so different from what appears on the surface,
the way we change as we move through the many facets

of our lives, the way being with someone else changes
the face we present to the world and all the while,
the secret face underneath. The sorrow is like the banging

of a broken muffler or the grief we carry like a cup filled
to the brim, a cup we try to balance in our hands, fearing
that if we were to spill it, if we were to let one drop fall,

we would not be able to stop, the way I could have cried
watching you hitch toward me, your belt pulled one
notch tighter, your leg dragging, the way you said

to my friend, "The second time I saw Maria,
it was at N.Y.U. I saw her ahead of me and she
was rushing. I had to run to catch up to her

and it's no different now." I remember that day,
at N.Y.U., when I heard you call my name
and I turned toward you. I could have taken wing

like this water chestnut, I was happy, standing
on that windy February corner, you blond
and young, your shoulders, broad and strong, your face lit.

How to Turn a Phone Call
into a Disaster

Sunday morning. Dennis has gone to church;
Because I don't have a workshop or a reading,
I am sitting on the sofa in my nightgown and robe.
I decide to call my son, and first my daughter-in-law
Answers; she sounds surprised that I called.
"Well," she says," I'm just going out. Here's John,"and then,

My son's voice. I ask how the children are, how Caroline
Is managing with her broken arm, and the front door bell rings.
"Oh, who's that?" I say, annoyed but moving to the front door
Holding the phone in my hand. My husband's friend is there,
Saying, "Get the walker. Dennis is having trouble."
I get flustered, as I always do in a crisis. "I'll call you back,"

I say, my voice shaking. I rush off to get the walker
With its little wheels, but I can't go outside. I'm still
In my soft slippers and it's raining. I watch Al
And his wife help Dennis up the walk, one on each arm,
Dennis embarrassed and struggling, each step achieved
After immense effort. Panic fills my chest like hundreds

Of mosquitoes. In the hall, the carpet catches in Dennis' feet,
And I shout "Stop, stop, you have to lift your feet," as though
He can help having his feet stuck to the floor. His body leans
Toward the walker as it slides away from him, his torso
Parallel with the floor. I lean over to pull his feet forward;
Only later do I realize that my fat thighs must have been
    visible
When I bent down. I get a chair for him; thank Al and his wife,
get Dennis a glass of water and his pills, my hands distraught
So I know I could never be a nurse or a doctor and I think
How terrible I am at this, and what a bad caretaker I'll make,

"What will I do? How will I manage?" I leave Dennis
Sitting in a chair in the living room waiting for his medicine

To work, and call John back. Before I get past, "Hello,"
I hear Dennis calling me, his voice tremulous. "Wait, John,
I have to see what he wants," and with the phone in my hand,
I run out to the living room where Dennis goes through an
Elaborate and slow explanation of how he wants me to ask
    John whether he uses
An electric razor and does it work and what kind does he use.

His friend uses a Norelco. What does John think?
It takes him ten minutes to say all this, as my mother-in-law
Used to say "To make a long story short," and she'd go on for
Two hours. He explains what I already understand; nervous
Laughter starts to bubble up into my chest. I rush back into
    the other room
And explain to John about the razor, and suddenly, I am
    sobbing and can't

Stop. I only cried like this, without restraint, maybe four times
    in my life,
But I can't stop and I can't get words out while my son is
    saying,
"Mom, what's the matter? What's the matter?" When I can
    speak again,
I say, "John, you needed this phone call like you needed a hole
In your head!" I've added one more worry to this son of mine
    who takes

Responsibility on his shoulders like an old man, though he is
    only thirty-four,
I try to make small talk, ask about his job, the children, the
    new house.
I can feel my composure crumbling, my voice starting to break
    apart again.
I think I could make a million dollars teaching people how to
    ruin
A person's day with a phone call.

This Morning

When the alarm goes off at 4:30, I leap out of bed
so I won't wake you and then I realize

you are already awake, your eyes staring
into darkness, your voice reedy and thin. You ask for a drink

of water and an Advil, and when I carry them to you, I see
that you are trembling, your eyes frightened.

"What is going to happen to me?" you ask.
I try to soothe you, try to find the words that will lull

you back onto the smooth lake of sleep, but the words
are fragile as paper boats. They cannot stay afloat.

I have to rush off, leaving you behind so I can be
in East Brunswick at 7 A.M., after driving

through the most congested areas in New Jersey,
cars snaking in a line ahead of me even this early.

Guilt washes over me for having chosen this life that takes
me away from you, while you lie in bed looking

like a slender child who needs to be held
and comforted. It is this image of you that I carry

as I drive down the Parkway and onto the New Jersey
Turnpike and onto Cranbury Road and into the high school

and into the classes where I read a poem about you
because a student asks me to. I tell them

about you, the image I cannot wash out of my head,
even though I know it is too sad for them. My mother

always said, "Young people shouldn't be told about
the troubles of adults. They'll have enough troubles

soon themselves." Their eyes say it's ok,
and they come up to talk to me. One young man

hands me a poem he wrote, others seem to need
to touch my arm or hand, and I am comforted

as I have not been comforted before.

Shame

Today I was thinking about shame and how much
it is a part of everything we do, about the way
I was ashamed at ten to say to my cousin
that my mother asked me to buy toilet paper,

as though my grown-up male cousin didn't use
toilet paper and wasn't stuck with all those messy bodily
functions we have to plan our lives around, the way public
bathrooms and our need for them remind us of our humanity,

a cosmic joke on us, so we won't forget how rooted we are
to the earth and not the ethereal beings the nuns wanted us
to be. Today I was thinking about shame and I see Dennis,
thin and frail and naked, the skin stretched tight over

his big bones, not an ounce of fat to cover him, the skin blue
and translucent, as he crawls from the bedroom on his
helpless legs to the bathroom. How ashamed he is,
as though this illness were a failure of his own manhood

and he to blame, how he pounds his fists on the floor in
frustration, how he scuttles into the bathroom and closes
the door after I see the dark well of sorrow in his eyes.
Today I am thinking about shame, and wish

it were only toilet paper or a red splotch on my dress
or my inability to learn the Periodic Table in Chemistry
that made me feel it, instead of my convoluted feelings
about my husband's illness, how nothing in our lives

is all one thing or another, not love, not grief, not anger,
but always mixed with its opposite emotion. I see Dennis
crawling along the floor, and I am struck with the axe of grief,
a terrible pity that can do no good, but mixed in with it,

the shame of my own impatience when he can't
remember something I told him two minutes ago,
or when he struggles for twenty minutes to open a package
and won't accept help, or when he insists he can walk

down the stairs and falls, the corrosive shame of my quick
annoyance, the shame of my lack of patience,
the shame of feeling that his illness is a deep
and muddy river in which we both will drown.

Donna Laura

Donna Laura, they called my grandmother
when they saw her sitting in the doorway, sewing
delicate tablecloths and linens, hours of sewing
bent over the cloth, an occupation for a lady.

Donna Laura, with her big house falling
to ruins around her head,
Donna Laura, whose husband
left for Argentina when she was twenty-four,
left her with seven children and no money
and her life in that southern Italian village
where the old ladies watched her
from their windows. She could not have
taken a breath without everyone knowing

Donna Laura who each day sucked
on the bitter seed
of her husband's failure
to send money and to remember
her long auburn hair,

Donna Laura who relied on the kindness
of the priest's "housekeeper"
to provide food for her family.
Everyone in the village knew

my grandmother's fine needlework
could not support seven children,
but everyone pretended not to see.

When she was ninety, Donna Laura
still lived in that mountain house.

Was her heart a bitter raisin,
her anger so deep it could have cut
a road through the mountain?
I touch the tablecloth she made,

the delicate scrollwork,
try to reach back to Donna Laura,
feel her life shaping itself into laced patterns
and scalloped edges from all those years between
her young womanhood and old age.

Only this cloth remains,
old and perfect still, turning her bitterness into art
to teach her granddaughters and great granddaughters
how to spin sorrow into gold.

Learning How to Love Myself

My hair is dark black and electric. Left to itself
it would spring off my head in ringlets. I could never

control it, not when I was growing up. It stuck out
from my head like a kinky tent. My legs are stumpy

and thick, the knees swollen, the veins protruding.
My small feet are wide and my body is planted

on the ground like a fat shrub. When I sit
on a high stool, I see my short, sturdy legs,

my thick body that carries me along,
unstoppable into my life, this peasant body.

For years, I longed for the slender grace
of a long body, tall and supple as marsh grass,

but would not give up this incredible energy,
the heat that pours from the furnace of my body,

the long line of women who taught me to laugh
my deep belly laugh and grab the world

in my arms and squeeze the sweetness out.

ALL THAT LIES BETWEEN US

2007

People Who Live Only in Photographs

My mantle is lined with photographs of the dead;
those people who live only in black and white.
Their faces, serious and self-contained, watch
sofas and chairs.

Dennis's great-grandmother and great-grandfather
stand in their Victorian wedding clothes: he, in his
stiff high-necked shirt, black suit; she, in her
high-necked gown, starched and pleated bodice,
plumed hat. They are not smiling, but look
prosperous and poised, a standard photo, circa 1892.

And here is Dennis's father as a young man
in his captain's uniform, a Bing Crosby look-alike.
He is pleased with himself and the world, next
to my father at sixteen in his first posed photograph,
proud and serious in his high-topped shoes,
dark suit and white collar, a formal bouquet
of flowers on the table. It is this photograph
his mother carried until she died, though he left
Italy when he was sixteen and never saw her again.

My grandmothers, whom I never met, stare
out of inexpensive frames. Beside Dennis's
grandmothers, who sit stately in their sterling
oval frames, they look poor and worn.

Looking at them, these people I see every day,
I think how little I know to tell a snippet of a story,
a name – nothing else. How little of their past
we can pass on to our own children and grandchildren.
My mother did piecework in a factory for fifty years,
sewing sleeves in coats for a few cents apiece.
I tried to piece together the past of these people

who exist now only in frames by asking questions,
but there is no one left to ask.

I wrote poems about my children as they grew up,
my mother and father, small bits I remembered
about my grandparents. I think now these poems are photos
of a past whose details otherwise no one would know.

Little House on the Prairie

After I found the *Little House on the Prairie*
books in the Riverside branch of the Paterson
Public Library, I read them all, my eyes moving
fast across the page, and then read them all
again, fascinated by the family's journey over mountains,
across plains, admiring the courage
it took to travel that huge emptiness to get
to a place they'd never been,

while I sat in Mr. Landgraff's seventh grade
at PS 18 in Paterson; Mr. Landgraff
who was sarcastic, mean, and handsome,
in a white-haired, white-man
kind of way. Mr. Landgraff who preferred
the pretty charming girls. Mr. Landgraff
who thought I was too introverted and shy.
I dreamt my way through seventh grade,
imagining myself in that covered wagon,
though I hadn't left Paterson more than twice,

for in *Little House* I found the bravery
I lacked, reading all evening at home
and walking to school in the morning,
sitting where Mr. Landgraff told me to sit,
crushable as a caterpillar. But after he marked
off my name in his attendance book, I floated
off to Kansas and Nebraska, sure that, like Laura,

I could be brave, that there was a place out there
where I could live a life as extraordinary
and risky as any I read about in books,
far removed from the chalk dust
and quiet despair of seventh grade
with its green black-out shades,

its picture of George Washington,
its scarred and battered desks
that tried to hold me captive.

What Did I Know About Love

I was twelve. What did I know about love,
about how I would love the boy
who lived next door
for being gentle and kind,
for the way he always acted
as if I were breakable and precious;
someone to be guarded and cared for,
though his father was a drunk
who beat him up, and his mother
was skinny with a cigarette always dangling
from the corner of her mouth.

Where did he learn such tenderness?
What un-smashed corner of himself carried
this sweetness? I think of him sometimes,
the first boy I ever loved, the one
who would be the model of every man
I ever fell for, with his golden hair, wide blue
eyes, clear skin, the long delicate fingers
of his hands, think and remember
how we'd walk home together

from PS 18 down the cracked and broken
sidewalks of 19th Street. One night, his family
moved out. "One step ahead of the bill collectors,"
the neighbors said. I did not see him again,
but I remember the way he'd stop a minute
at my house to watch me head toward
our back stoop, and then he'd turn,
face his own house and hesitate,
gathering himself to go inside.

The Mediterranean

At twenty-three, my mother followed my father
to Paterson from San Mauro, that small town
that clung to a mountaintop. From her window
in that southern Italian village, she glimpsed
the Mediterranean, glistening blue.

In the village, they heard stories of storms
that rose from the sea, swallowed fishermen
and boats. As a child, she heard them,
but loved the sea anyway, her own secret
jewel with its incredible light.

In Paterson, inside our tenement, my mother made
the food she'd grown up cooking, filled the house
with the unforgettable aroma of Mediterranean cuisine,
told us stories of San Mauro, the stone house

where she lived, the well where they drew
their water, the stream where they washed their clothes,
the fields built like steps up the sides of the mountain,
but it was the sea she most remembered.

When she spoke of that huge horizon,
sky scrubbed clean by salt air,
sand white as a bleached handkerchief,
we saw the Mediterranean through my mother's eyes,

vivid flowers of Italian summers always with us.

Christmas Story

My mother didn't believe in toys,
felt they were frills we couldn't afford anyway.
I don't remember ever being given a doll
or any other toy. We had paper dolls, one
or two books of them, and games – cards,
dominoes, Monopoly because we could play
these together: my mother wanted us
to be friends, to stay on our front stoop
where she could keep her eye on us,
but Christmas presents in our house were white cotton
underpants, undershirts, socks. She didn't intend
to be cruel. In Italy, by the time she was seven,
she was cooking for the family – all nine
of them – cleaning the house,
tending the chickens and pigs.
Children had to grow up, no time to waste
on toys, but she wanted us to be happy.
Sometimes when she went downtown
to pay five dollars a week on time
for our refrigerator, she'd bring us a box
of imitation M&M's from Kresge's.
They came in a clear plastic box, bright colors
shining through. We'd try to make them last
because, when they were gone, a new box
might not appear for a month or even two.
We used the boxes as couches for our paper
dolls or runways for pretend cars
made of empty spools of thread,
and we'd make up stories, lying
on the floor between the wall
and the bed. I think of my own children,
how I nearly drowned them in presents
at Christmas: GI Joe and Barbie, tanks
and trucks and Legos and blocks, Barbie's

Dream House and Barbie's Convertible,
Barbie's Shore House and Ken,
as though the child that still lives inside me
could fill those Christmas mornings
with more than plain white underwear.

There Was No Pleasing My Mother

Even the things I did well got on her nerves.
Tobias Wolff

My mother found fault with everything
about me, my wild hair, my sloppiness,

my desire to read books, my children
and the way I raised them. "Imagine,"

she said, "letting children run barefoot
in the house. Why they might step

on a needle," despite the fact
that I didn't sew, so it was unlikely

I'd be able to find a needle to step on
even if I wanted to. She even blamed me

for the cat who'd leap off the couch
and hide as soon as he heard her

enter the house. It's not that she didn't
love me and show it in a hundred ways,

but that I was only safe when I was home,
like the day, shortly after I got engaged,

when I was at a girlfriend's house
with five other girls. It started to snow,

and though my girlfriend's house was ten blocks
from my own, my mother called up and said,

"Come home. It's snowing. You're going to lose
your ring." We laughed so hard, my friends and I,

that, as soon as the laughter died down,
we'd start again, and for years they all teased me,

"Come home. It's snowing. You'll lose your ring."
They'd mimic my mother's deeply accented voice,

and I'd laugh too, though part of me didn't
believe I could do anything without her.

Breakfast at IHOP

This morning, I watch the somber man sit
alone at a nearby table, book open before him,
two place settings. He takes out
his cell phone and dials. I hear his half

of the conversation and try not to look
at him because I see his friend has forgotten
him. His voice stutters as they make another
appointment to meet. He tells the waitress

his friend won't be joining him and orders.
I remember the party I was invited to in sixth
grade, that grade when Judy, my best friend
since we were three, found other girls

to be her friends, outgoing girls, pretty girls,
girls who knew how to talk and laugh
with boys the way she did. I ran home
after school on the day of the party.

I left Judy at her house with Diane and Camille.
"I'll wait for you," I said.
I looked out the front window and waited
with my present wrapped in inexpensive paper,

but they never picked me up like they promised.
In that man's face, I see the same shame I felt
that day, to have been forgotten, left behind,
to be so unimportant even your friends

don't remember you.

Vestal, New York

I Want to Write a Poem to Celebrate

my father's arms, bulging and straining while he carries
the wooden box of purple grapes down the crumbling,

uneven cement steps into the cellar of the old house
on 19th Street. The cellar, whitewashed by my mother,

grows darker as my father lumbers past the big coal
furnace and into the windowless wine room

at the back where he will feed the grapes,
ripe and perfect and smelling of earth,

into the wine press. The grape smell changes
as they are crushed and drawn out into fat

wooden barrels, and for weeks the cellar
will be full to the brim with the sweet smell

of grapes fermenting into wine, a smell I recognize
even forty years later each time I uncork a bottle,

an aroma that brings back my father
and his friends gathering under Zio Gianni's

grape arbor to play briscole through long July
nights, small glasses before them, peach slices

gleaming like amber in the ruby wine.

Superman

Superman was my brother's hero: Clark Kent with his
horn-rimmed glasses, just like my brother's, transformed
into someone who could leap tall buildings
in a single bound, and Lois Lane who loved him.

This was 1950s TV and the girl was always
the foil for the hero, the one who helped
but never took center stage. I never wanted
to be like that. I wanted to be the one

who made things happen, though there were no
super girls in 1950. This was right after the war,
and when the men came home, they wanted
their jobs back, wanted their women in aprons

to put their dinners on the table as soon
as they walked in the door. I'd seen
my mother in her homemade apron
struggling to cook everything from scratch,

cooking and canning and cleaning.
This didn't appeal to me, though
I knew I would marry. I was supposed
to marry. Everyone did. But when I graduated

from high school I knew what I didn't want:
to be married and pregnant like some
of my girlfriends, right before they graduated,
or right after. I didn't want to go .

to William Paterson College as my mother wished,
to be a kindergarten teacher so I could be at home
when my children had finished their days at school.
"I want to go to college, be a writer,"

I announced, not listening when my accountant cousin
said this was the most impractical ambition he'd ever
heard of. "I want to be a writer," knowing
that I would never play Lois Lane to a Superman.

Tenacious as a bulldog, I kept trying, even
though I knew my cousin was right. It was
an impractical ambition, but one I couldn't trade
for any other, since words were the way

I could leap tall buildings in a single bound.

I Am Thinking of the Dress

I am thinking of the dress I wore
to my senior prom, pale blue chiffon

with a nipped-in waist and a swirly skirt
that cost more money than my mother

could afford but bought for me
anyway, even though pale blue

is not a good color for a dark-skinned girl,
but rather for the girl I wished I could be.

I wore that dress with high heels and nylons,
garter belt and a lace bra. I went to the prom

with Jimmy, the boy I dated senior year,
a boy I didn't love and who didn't love me.

The prom was at the North Jersey Country Club,
and after dinner, the couples scattered

out to the grounds, couples draped
on the lounge chairs around the pool. Lois

and Bill, our best friends, went into the woods.
When they came back Lois's dress was stained

and crumpled and they acted proud of themselves.
Jimmy and I walked around the pool. He held

my hand. We sat on a bench and he kissed me
and kissed me and nothing happened – no spark

at all. I think of him now, poor Jimmy,
trying so hard to make people think

he was straight, like me sitting on that stone
bench in my beautiful blue dress

trying to make people believe
I could get a handsome date.

My Father's Fig Trees
in Hawthorne, New Jersey

Each winter, my father wrapped his fig trees
in burlap and buried them; each spring

he lifted them out of the earth and unwrapped
them. How they turned toward the sun

in their flowering, grew hundreds of fat purple
fruit that my father picked each day,

washing them off and presenting them to me
as though they were diamonds or pearls.

I paid people to empty my parents' house
of fifty years of accumulation, to sell

their things to the first bidder. I hid
from the task of packing and sorting,

each item a reminder. This one last thing
I could have done in their honor

was too much, the guilt and shame
twin scarves I wear for the place that broke

inside me when I couldn't manage
and hid in my bed for weeks.

I pass my parents' house and want
to stop, to walk into the small backyard

to see if the fig trees are still there.
I could not manage to find someone

to dig up the trees, replant them at my house
and, instead, left them for people

who do not know how much of that Italian
mountain village my father left

when he was sixteen was in that rich fruit,
the earthy sweetness of it, the way my father

did not eat the figs himself, but always
saved them for me.

My Sister and Frank Sinatra

My cousin says, "You're the last person alive
from my childhood," and we both nearly begin

to cry, two ladies heading out for lunch
in my cousin's sleek new convertible. Before

she starts the car she hands me
an old photograph. At the forefront

my sister looks out at the camera.
In the photo she is twenty-five,

just married. I had forgotten
how exquisitely beautiful she was as a girl,

her full sensuous lips, her large chocolate brown
eyes, the sweetheart curve of her Elizabeth

Taylor face, her Marilyn Monroe body.
Waves of energy came off her. By the time

she died at sixty-two, crippled in a wheelchair,
she struggled against the narrowing

frame of her life, retreated gradually
away from us, ashamed of her twisted

and crooked hands, her feet
so distorted that she had to wear ugly shoes

specially made for her. When she was a girl,
legs slender, size-five feet beautifully formed,

she loved to dance in high heels,
twirling around the dance floor doing the rhumba

and the jitterbug. We'd listen to Sinatra when we'd ride
around in my cousin's used car, an old black Ford:

my sister, her friend Florence, and my cousin,
riding out of constricted Paterson streets

to the wider country lanes of Bergen County.
We thought it would be as easy as that,

our lives utterly changed if we found the man
we longed for, the love Sinatra made us sure

was real. We were the Happily Ever After Girls,
believed in that myth like we believed nothing else.

I hold my sister's picture in my hand, feel the
weight of that past, those 1950s girls, the way

happiness is water you can't hold in your hands.
We didn't know then that, like our mothers,

those women we vowed we'd never be,
we'd end up making do with whatever

presented itself before us.

Sunday Dinners at My Mother's House

After I was grown up and had a house
and a family of my own, my mother cooked
and served dinner for all of us, her children
and grandchildren, at least sixteen people
each Sunday in her basement kitchen.
My mother was an artist of food,
and we gathered around three tables lined up,
end to end, macaroni and meatballs, braciola,
salad and roasted chicken, potatoes and stuffed
artichokes, fruit and nuts with their own silvery
nutcrackers, apple pies and turnovers,
espresso and anisette.

Every Sunday the courses emerged from that kitchen
and arrived at the table as if by magic: my mother,
moving like a dervish between the kitchen
and the finished room that was our cellar
dining room in that tiny house, that wouldn't hold
all of us in the dining room upstairs. The upstairs
kitchen, clean and untouched, was almost never used,
except to serve coffee to guests we didn't know well,
while the family and friends all gathered in the cellar
to eat and talk politics and baseball: the cousins,
whispering and giggling at the end table,
and the rest of us as excited and loud as a convention
of beer salesmen, except for my brother, the doctor,
always soft-spoken. My father and I,
the political radicals, the loudest of all
in our convictions.

My father, at ninety-two, asked me to take him
in his wheelchair to march on Washington.
"The people are asleep," he said.
"We have to try to wake them up."
My mother didn't care about politics at all;
she only cared about us, about keeping us
all close to her and together.
"When you have trouble," she said,
"only your family will help you,"
and we all came back to be near her,
back to that blue-collar town where she lived,
my sister's house across the street from mine,
my brother's on top of the hill,
my mother's not five minutes away.
I'd see her smiling, happy that we were all
together, willing to cook for all of us, week
after week, to make sure we'd stay that way.

In my mother's kitchen, there were always
stories and laughter, arguments and excitement.
When I was nineteen I went to a friend's house
for dinner. It was the first time I sat at a table
where no one spoke, no stories or conversation
or laughter, only pass the potatoes please,
the mother sitting stiff as a stick at one end
of the table, the father at the other, his mouth
a staple in his somber face. I was glad to go home.

Now it is ten years since my mother died,
four since my father's death, two since my sister's.
My son and his family are in North Carolina;
my daughter in Cambridge; my brother's son in Chicago.
I remember my father saying when my son moved
away, not a year after my mother was dead,
"Without your mother the chain is broken."

My Father Always Drove

My father always drove. My mother sat
in the passenger seat giving directions,
advising him when to turn or when to slow
down, though it's hard to imagine him driving
any slower. His top speed was ten miles an hour,
even in that bright red Ford he bought secondhand,

the one my mother was so upset about.
After his old blue Chevy collapsed,
he had to pay someone to take it away.
He went off with one of his friends
to look at used cars and drove into our

driveway in that bright red Ford.
My mother thought the car called
attention to itself, and never climbed
into that car without telling my father
what she thought of it. But it took her

where she had to go: grocery shopping,
doctor's office, grandchildren-sitting
on Friday nights. It took my father
to visit his friends where he played cards
and talked politics. My father always drove.

All her kindergarten year, while I taught
college, he took my daughter to school
and picked her up, taught her to play cards
with him; her face, concentrated and serious,

above the Queen of Hearts and Jacks.
My father drove that red car
until he was eighty-six. Everyone
in town knew him, the old guy
who drove five miles an hour

through the center of town,
always ready to bring us,
his children and grandchildren,
a gift, a paper sack of fresh figs

from his trees, tomatoes from the garden,
chocolate candies for the children, silver dollars
he'd saved, lottery tickets he hoped would win
us a million. Even our cat knew him.

The cat would sit on the front porch watching.
When my father would turn the corner
onto Oak Place, the cat would leap off
the porch and race down the street
toward him, following the car to the house

and following my father inside. My father arrived,
carrying a foil-wrapped package of liver or fish,
happy to give gifts, even to this cat,
who purred for him.

Spike-Heels

In the 1950s, I wore spike-heels.
They were very high, but I was thin then,

didn't wobble. I walked through hours
at my job, my high heels twinkly

as Dorothy's red slippers with pointy toes,
heels in every possible color, sling-backs

and pumps, the clickety-clack of them
on pavement making me feel

as sophisticated as Marilyn Monroe. Older now,
my heels have gone lower and lower,

reduced to sandals with Velcro straps to hold
my triple E-feet. I still watch women

striding in their spike-heels, and wish
for one minute that I could go back

to the days when I could walk
with such grace, look with longing

at this marker of beauty, as though
I were still sixteen and not this woman

I've become, pounding through life
on confident feet.

Trying to Get You to Love Me

When we were young, I made lists of ways
to get you to love me. I'd try to make you

jealous by talking about the places I'd gone,
though I didn't mention the name

of the other man I was dating. Your friend Paul,
whom I hated because he was obnoxious

and seemed to control you, told you
that going out on Saturday night was

cliché. So you'd take me out on Friday
or Sunday, which worked out well for me

because I went out with Frank on Tuesday
and Saturday. Frank squired me to expensive

restaurants in New Jersey and to dinner theater
and took me on long drives into New York State

where we'd eat at an expensive restaurant
and drive back home. He told me

how he made a million dollars by buying
a farm from a farmer one afternoon

and selling it to someone else an hour
later for forty times the amount

he'd paid, and about a housing development
he was building in Mahwah. He took me

through the model home, told me
he'd save sixty-five dollars a house

because he'd put in a counter rather than
a vanity with shelves and doors.

You took me to New York City to hear
folk singers like Pete Seeger, and to the Cloisters,

the Botanical Gardens and the Bronx Zoo.
Once on the way home from a drive

into New York State, Frank stopped the car
at a lookout and began to kiss me

and to try to take my blouse off. I told him
I couldn't, that I had to go home. When you

and I parked at Palisades Park on the edge
of the cliffs with the New York view,

I would have done anything you asked.
I thought you were beautiful, the prototype

of every man I'd ever loved with your blond
hair, blue eyes, high cheekbones and light skin,

the opposite of all the Italian boys I knew.
But I didn't know whether you loved me

or thought me beautiful. I looked at *Seventeen*
magazine and *Mademoiselle*, tried to read

all the articles about how to get a man, but still
I was never sure. One day I said I'd been

to Trader Vic's in New York City (with Frank,
of course, but I didn't say that), and you started

shouting at me. "I don't know what you're doing,"
you said. "Do you love me, or not?" I tried to explain,

to say that I didn't know what you felt,
that you never asked me to go steady,

never talked about anything more
than our next date. By the end of the evening,

we were engaged. I told Frank the next day
that I couldn't see him anymore. He was furious

and, for two years, he refused to talk to my friend
who introduced us. I didn't care. Though I felt

a little guilty, mostly I could see the lives ahead
of us in Technicolor, the wedding cake,

the honeymoon, the house and children,
and you, the man I loved and married.

Housework and Buicks with Fins

When we were first married, Dennis bought a
1957 Buick, pale blue and white, with huge fins

to replace the dilapidated brown Pontiac
he used to drive. I owned a Sapphire blue

Volkswagen, with a sun roof, which was easy
to maneuver in and out of spaces.

It was the only car I'd ever driven.
When I looked at Dennis's Buick, I couldn't

imagine how I'd steer that yacht of a car down
the crowded streets of Hawthorne and Paterson.

One day my car was being repaired and I had
to take Dennis's car to run an errand,

but, when I got to the store and tried to
parallel park, I couldn't manage and had to go

back home. I pulled into the driveway
of the small Cape Cod house we bought before

we were married, the house that *I* bought
because I had saved enough money for a down-

payment. My sister and mother and I had
scrubbed the filthy floors in that house

with Brillo because it was the only way
to get it clean, and we painted it and threw out

the junk the former owners left behind. I
realize now that Dennis didn't help at all,

though I don't know why it didn't occur to me
then, nor did I realize that I was setting up

a pattern for the way things would be, married
to my 1950s husband who expected me to be

the 1950s wife he thought he'd married, both of us
babied by our mothers, mine who poured my

milk and buttered my toast until the day I left,
and his mother who served all his meals

to him in the dining room so that he had never
cleaned a pan or cooked a meal for himself.

We had a wild first six months of marriage. I was
waiting for him to serve me, he was waiting for

me to serve him, until finally I realized what I
should have known before the wedding march

and white gown, should have known when
I was on my hands and knees scrubbing

that floor – if anything was going to get done,
I'd have to do it myself, all except driving

that huge Buick. That I left to him.

Driving into Our New Lives

Years ago, driving across the mountains
in West Virginia, both of us are so young
we don't know anything. We are twenty-eight
years old, our children sleeping in the back seat.
With your fresh Ph.D. in your suitcase, we head out
toward Kansas City. We've never been anywhere.
We decide to go the long way around
instead of driving due west.

Years ago, driving across mountains, your
hand resting on my knee, the radio playing the folk
music we love, Pete Seeger, Joan Baez, or you
singing songs to keep the children entertained.
How could we know what is to come?

We are young. We think we'll be healthy
and strong forever. We are certain we are invincible
because we love each other, because our children
are smart and beautiful, because we are heading

to a new place, because the stars
in the coal-black West Virginia sky are so thick,
they could be chunks of ice.
How could we know what is to come?

Nighties

At my bridal shower, someone gave me
a pink see-through nightgown and pink satin
slippers with slender heels and feathers.
The gown had feathers on it too.

I've always hated my legs and even then,
when I was still thin and in good shape,
I didn't want to wear that nightgown
or slippers, didn't want to parade

in front of you like some pin-up.
But I wore them anyway, all those negligées
I got as shower presents, sleazy nylon
I didn't know was tacky. When I wore

shorty nightgowns, I'd leap into bed
not wanting you to notice how
the nightgown revealed what I thought
my biggest flaw. In all the young years

of our marriage, I wore a different nightgown
every night, not that it ever stayed on for long,
and afterwards I'd pull it back on, afraid
our children would find me naked in our bed.

I felt so sophisticated in those nightgowns,
like the ones Doris Day wore in movies.
Only years later, when my daughter buys me
a nightgown made of soft and smooth blue silk,

do I realize that the first ones I owned
were cheap imitations of this, the one
I hold now to my cheek, grateful
to have been once what I was.

How lucky I am to have loved you
in nylon, silk, my own incredible skin.

In the Movies No One Ever Ages

I wish I could say the same for me,
but that's what's so wonderful about the movies.
The people on the screen remain as they were,
yet for me, when I look back at our lives,
you too are caught in freeze-frame, light
coming off you, the planes of your handsome
face, your perfect, muscular body.
Do you remember walking through
the New York Botanical Gardens?
You, your mind filled with facts
like an encyclopedia, your photographic
memory, told me all about the flowers
and birds and the trees inside the towering
greenhouses. We walked and kissed behind
the exuberant vegetation of the African rainforest,
tropical birds skimming the air above our heads.

Do you remember the concert
at Columbia too and how exciting
it was to hear Pete Seeger sing in person?
We walked together across that moonlit campus.
These moments are what I hold now when
I see you struggling to win against a disease
that has robbed you of almost everything.
Each day is one less thing you can do,
though you can still hold my hand,
put your frail arms around me.

Who Knew How Lonely
the Truth Can Be

When I was still timid and shy I hated
people who told the truth, bluntly,

blurting out that you had a big nose
or that your shampoo smelled cheap. Then

I studied Keats and his claim that poetry
is truth and beauty and I had no idea

what he was talking about until I was forty
years old and saw how truth in a poem

makes the hair on the back of my neck rise.
Now, when I am the one blurting out truths that

often leave people staring, when I say at my
department meeting the very thing that others won't,

how alone I become as I speak, a space
cleared around me as though I have

the plague. That loneliness I can stand. The other
loneliness, the truth we can barely admit to ourselves

at three A.M. when we're lying in bed unable
to sleep, that truth, the one too ugly to admit,

how we want to climb to the top of a tower
and shake off all the arms that need

our comfort and the way we need
to be selfish, to climb into that tower

and not let down our hair, to be
for at least a little while

only for ourselves,
selfish and quiet and alone.

I Wish I Knew How to Tell You

My fear the other night, the night
when we went out to dinner
and I hauled you in your collapsible
wheelchair to the restaurant
where we had dinner so many times
when you could still walk

you so frail looking and nervous
because your arms flap around
like angry birds, and you knock
things off the table,
sure that people are looking at you.
"It's getting worse," you say. "I'm scared."
I hear your words and think

how caught we are in our own skins,
how hard it is to feel what someone else
feels. I think I'm sympathetic. I think I'm kind.
I want to believe that,
but, when we get home, I get violently sick

from food poisoning, shivering so badly
I can't keep my hands still, my teeth chattering.
Finally, after heaving for an hour,
I wrap myself in quilts and get into bed,
this physical assault making my arthritis
flare up so I can't bend my knee

or put my feet on the floor, or move my back
or my hand without pain, and I say to you
who hover around me, "Please leave the door open."
I don't say, "I'm afraid, I don't want to be alone,"
but that's what I mean, and for the first time I,
who am always on the road, my sturdy body

taking me everywhere like a dependable car,
really understand what you feel when you come
to me in your electric wheelchair, the *scrich scrich*
of its wheels on the carpet, your hands trembling,
your face pale and perspiring, your eyes avoiding mine.
"I'm afraid," you say. "Hold my hand."

What a Liar I Am

I have been lying for a long time now,
the sicker you get the more I lie
to myself most of all. I cannot say
how angry I am that this illness
is another person in our house, so lies
are the only way to get through each day.

How hard it is to admit that I am often
impatient and raging and that anger
is a pit I can never swallow, that love,
even mine for you who have been with me
forty years, cannot dissolve the hank
of loneliness that has become lodged

in my throat, the irritating squeaking
of your electric wheelchair, the way
I want to run from the putrid smell
of medicines rising from your skin,
the way I lie and lie so you won't know

how heavy this illness feels. How long
it has been going on, sixteen years now.
Your feet, dragging along the carpet
on days you can still walk,
are like a fingernail on a blackboard.
"This is all too much for you," you say,
and I reassure you, "No, not for you,

nothing is too much for you."
"I am a burden," you say,
and "No, no," I say. "Not a burden."
The face I see in my mirror is not one
I want to see. O love, I could not
have imagined it would come to this,

when I can only live by lying to myself
and you, you with your begging eyes,
your reedy voice, a clanging bell that calls me,
you whom I love but cannot carry.

On an Outing to Cold Spring

In the photograph my arm is around your waist,
my head leans against your shoulder, the sun washes
your hair in light. In the background a cardboard
cut-out of a beautiful Victorian lady in a straw hat
watches us, a scowl on her face.
We do not see her. The picture captures
the frozen look of the muscles of your face,
though you still look handsome. The disease
has only just begun to take hold. We are
on an outing to Cold Spring Harbor.
You have no trouble walking. I convince myself
this is as bad as it will be.
The woman behind us knows more than I do.

Yesterday, I go to the lawyer who advises me
to get a bed and board divorce or, she says,
"You will be impoverished." I am so nervous
when she speaks to me that I have to
keep asking her to repeat what she is saying
so I can write it down. "Look," she says, "he
isn't going to get better, only worse.
You have to try to protect yourself." Later,
I sit with you, explain what she advised,
try to keep my voice from splitting apart
and you say, "I want you to be safe.
A divorce," you say, and your hands shake.
"Only a bed and board divorce –
not a real divorce," I say.

In the lawyer's office, her conference room with its
exposed brick walls, her framed Van Gogh posters,
her handmade antique quilt hanging on the walls,
she asks what your condition is now. I explain.
She says, "The law allows you to do this."

In our family room, you sit next to me
in your wheelchair. You reach out
to touch my face. I hold you and stare
over your shoulders at this picture
of us, standing in that garden, oblivious
to how much it is possible to lose,
and I know the subtext in this script,
that today we are admitting
that you are racing downhill
like an out-of-control sled,
and nothing I can do will stop you.

Selective Memory

Our daughter tells me I practice selective
memory, that I erase the parts of the past
I don't like or don't want to know.
I denied it, but then I thought maybe
she was right after all, that maybe I need
to soften the sharp edges of memory, as though
I were working colored chalk over a painting.

So it must have been selective memory
that I was practicing when I let myself
forget that I've always loved my husband
more than he loved me, that fact I forced
myself to forget as he grew ill and we grew
together over the years, moments glittering
like gold in rock, the way those remembered
glimpses of a beloved face, or the feel
of a hand or words spoken softly stay
with us and run like a vein through the lives
of couples like us, long married and happy
together, our lives growing to fit us
like another skin,

and it must be selective memory that makes me
remember the explosion of love between us and not
the anger with which we fought when we were
young and before you got sick.

One night, sitting in our bed, I am raving
and furious that my friend who cried
at his wife's funeral two months ago
is already going dancing each night.
I say, "He'll probably be married within six months,"
and you say, "If something happened to you I
would remarry, why not?" And your words sting worse

than if you had slapped me, who wanted – no,
expected – to hear that you wouldn't want anyone
but me, even if you were lying, the kind
of lie we all tell to protect those we love,
and "I can't believe you," I say,
and you say, "Why not? Why not?"
And I think that our daughter is right,
that I practice selective memory. I am angry
thinking of you, like my friend spending
his wife's money on someone else,
and I wish you had lied to me
as I lie to you so often
to protect you.

For a moment I see you in your electric
wheelchair dancing around the room
with another woman, passing my money
on to her instead of our children
and grandchildren. I cannot believe
how furious I am.

For a few days I don't let my pity
for you touch my heart, and then
we are watching the debates together:
you in your wheelchair and me
on the sofa. I watch you, your face
twitching and moving, your neck twisting,
your arms jerking, and I remember
how much I love you, and would,
even if you married someone else,
even if I had to return from my grave
to haunt you, even then, I can't help
the tenderness I still feel
when I look at you.

Your Voice on the Phone Wobbles

Your voice on the phone wobbles and sounds tight
as one of the strings of your guitar,

the one you used to play when you could
still sing. From my motel room, I try

to smooth away your shaking, as I would
if I were at home with you, smoothing

my hand across your shoulders until the muscles
unknot. "Where are you?" I ask,
and you say you're upstairs at your

computer. I can tell you are frantic
because the message you're trying to send

to the Computer Help Line keeps
getting erased. Your hands no longer work

the way you want them to. I am afraid
you will fall downstairs in your distraction,

the woman who helps you already gone.
Last week you insisted you could walk.

It was only ten in the morning, and you said
you could always walk until at least 11:30.

I drove you to the drugstore. We walked inside.
I got a cart for you to lean on,

but you didn't want it. I left you standing
in an aisle looking for shaving lotion.

I was looking at the rows of cough
medicine and cold remedies when I heard

a crash. I rushed into the next aisle
and found you struggling to get up

from the floor. I helped you up,
tried to talk you into leaning

on the cart. You refused. Two minutes later,
you fell again, the way you do, as though

you were a felled tree. I pretended
people weren't staring at us. Tonight

with your voice so ragged, I try to talk
you into going downstairs to your chair,

try to get you to give up on the computer
and read a book. I feel like your

mother, scolding, prodding. I don't know
the exact day or year when things changed

like this between us. They say in each
relationship the person who loves the most

gives all the power to the one who doesn't
love as much. I was besotted with you,

bent myself to your will. Maybe it was this
illness, your need of me suddenly greater

than mine for you, that made me seem
more valuable, more cherished,

so I can tell that two days since
I left home you need me back, the way

you never would have needed me then.

On Thanksgiving This Year

Two days before Thanksgiving I take you
to a Parkinson's Research Center
where the doctor says you are over-
medicated and cuts back on medicine
by thirty percent. You start the regimen
the next day and, by Thanksgiving,
you are having so much trouble moving,
Jennifer and I take you across the street
in your collapsible wheelchair and lift
you out of it and onto my niece's sofa.
When we help you to the table, I watch
you turning into an old man on some
pill that works the opposite of the fountain
of youth, your head bends forward
so your chin touches your chest
and you are incomprehensible
when you try to speak.
Your fork falls from your hand
when you try to lift it. I watch you struggle,
ask in a whisper if I can help you.
"No," you say, "no, I need to go home."
We lift you into the wheelchair
and your body looks like the body
of a ninety-year-old man,
though you are only sixty-five.
At home again, you are unable
to eat your dinner. You have an accident.
Jennifer and I struggle to get your wet
clothes off and put on clean clothes,
and that happens three times,
and by the third time I am about to cry.
You say, "Shoot me. Please shoot me."
"Don't worry," I say.
"Don't worry, it will be okay."

And then Jennifer takes over
and says, "Go sit down for a minute."
She changes you again.
You cry. Finally, we put you to bed
with a book, prop the book up for you
because your hands won't hold it. In the middle
of the night, I, who sleep like the dead, don't
hear you call, and Jennifer gets up to help
you out of bed to use the urinal. In the morning,
I finally reach the neurologist who says,
"That's called a crash. They used
to put PD patients in the hospital
when they cut back these drugs."
He says to put you back on the medicine
and we do. Gradually you come back
to yourself, and though it's not good,
you're not totally paralyzed. But the image
of you incontinent, frozen, is the elephant
in the room with us, the one I try to ignore,
though I know it's there. "Have you
taken care of the money?" you ask.
"You know – don't you? – that I'm going to be
like that by the end of next year."

I Never Tell People

I never tell people that I almost left you
twenty years ago, don't tell them how your rage

terrified me when I watched you pick up
the sugar bowl and hurl it at the wall,

don't tell them about the summer we painted
the bedrooms and you screamed and screamed

out the open windows until I yelled back
and the neighbors came out to water their lawns

so they could hear, don't tell them about
the time you were so angry at me

that we fought on the stairs and you punched
me and I punched back. I shouted, "I want

a divorce," and you went totally still
and said, "No, no, I won't give you one,"

and then you said, "See. I knew you never
loved me." I took the keys and drove around

Bergen County for hours. When I came back
it was getting dark and we tiptoed

around each other, afraid of the chasm
that had opened between us. In our bed

that night, after the children fell asleep,
you got me back the way you always did,

sex, the way you soothed my hurt feelings,
the bruises on my arms where you punched me,

the way you whistled in the shower after
the latest argument had lost the power

to harm. I never tell anyone how I blamed
myself for the broken places inside you.

I tried to stay out of the way when you slapped
your own face or banged your head on the wall

for losing a pencil or a notebook or to escape
your father's voice inside you listing all your flaws.

So how then did I come to this place where
I knew I wasn't to blame, that I had to save

what I needed for myself, to keep your fists
from smashing what I was? After all

the arguments, screaming, I stopped feeling
so frightened of your fury. I never tell

anyone that twenty years ago I almost left
you, the two of us caught in the tornado

of your flailing arms, flailing like the way
they move uncontrollably now with your disease,

and found instead this quiet place where you,
the man I hated and loved, are the boat

I rock in each night, almost forgetting
those turbulent years when the sadness

you carried like a rotten tooth in your mouth,
the empty places I could never fill,

nearly broke us.

Do You Know What It Is I Feel?

By evening now, often you can't walk, your thin
frame falling into your electric wheelchair,
the *knuck knuck* of its wheels on the hardwood
floors, the bang and clatter of it hitting
the French doors or the refrigerator,
or scraping along the mahogany furniture
your mother left us.

You finally arrive next to the sofa where
I am curled under the Victorian velvet throw
our daughter gave me. Your chair pulled up
close to the sofa arm, you reach out
for my hand and hold it while we watch
a movie together, my eyes sliding sideways
and looking at you. It's too difficult

to confront you head on, your body growing
thinner with each day, your neck suddenly
too weak to hold up your head. I remember
you when we were young, look at the picture
on the shelf behind us, of you
on the camping trip we took to Swartswood Lake,
you holding the flap of the tent open

for our two-year-old daughter with her blond
ringlets and violet eyes. You look so beautiful
in the dappled light, your shoulders wide
and muscular, your narrow waist, the muscles
of your legs sharply defined against your jeans.
I'd look at you, and my breath

would catch in my throat. Now, when
I look at you, pity is a knife that
cuts me through. The trips I thought we'd take,
the places we'd see together, the old age
I'd imagined has vanished and instead I have,
these few hours when I hold your hand

and don't dare look at you too closely
for fear I will have to know how angry I am
that you have left me when I still have need.

What I Remember

Hot Ovaltine in the 17th Street kitchen
with its scrubbed linoleum and steaming farina.
The coal stove spilling its heat over my back;
the loose windows patterned with ice,
my mother serving us, my mother who rarely
said, "I love you," but showed it
with each stirring
of her cooking pots and spoons.

My father cracked eggs into a thick-sided cup
and stirred them with sugar, making
a ceremony out of handing me the eggs
that were supposed to keep me, his skinny,
weak-chested daughter, from getting sick again.

That kitchen, the soft light of the etched-glass fixture,
the oil cloth-covered table, is that place
I return to when the thought of you
is suddenly too much for me to carry,
this suitcase full of fear, when all my running,
the readings and workshops and lectures and friends
won't allow me to forget.

If I don't think about it, maybe I can
get you back the way you were and not
the shaking voice you have become,
who tells me on the phone last night,
"It's getting worse. Soon I won't be able
to move at all and then what will happen?"
Though I soothe you, my shame is
that I am not with you when you hallucinate
the tie of your robe is a snake or the socks
you left on the floor are mice.

I would take us both back
to the 17th Street kitchen, pull you
into my memory of that place so filled
with soft light and arms that held me.
My father could stir an egg for you
in a cup. My mother break off a piece
of hot bread for you; spread butter on it
from the Lakeview Dairy crock the milkman
delivered. My sister and brother could help
us bake sugar cookies. We could play Monopoly.
We could leave all our grief in a sack by the door.

I Walk Through the Rooms
of Memory

I walk through the rooms of memory, counting
my dead. First, my mother with her quick laugh
and her energy and her earthy humor, old wise
woman, who leaves a hole in the center

of my days larger than Times Square;
then, my father with his love of company
and his open heart and his radical politics.
And, finally, my sister who always knew

the quickest way to get something done,
all of them lost to me now. All the rooms
of memory are full of dust, and words
spoken years ago in anger or sorrow festoon

the windows. The voices, that is what remains,
their voices bring them back to me. I see
my mother serving me espresso and cake
at her kitchen table, the one in the basement,

metal with plastic-covered metal chairs,
my mother saying, "I don't have anything
to give you to eat," and then opening the door
of the old Kelvinator and producing pasta

and fagoli or chicken and fish, meatballs
and homemade bread, my mother who never cried
or said, "I love you," but showed it
in everything she did, and my father

sitting at ninety-two in his brown recliner
from Medicare, his shrinking body
overshadowed by the chair meant for someone
so much bigger than he. And Laura, I remember

you as we were when we were girls, you
with your size thirty-six D breasts that men
always wanted to touch and your hourglass
figure and your slender legs and beautiful

size-five feet, you with your big smile

and your perfect teeth, you in your Fire-and-Ice
lipstick, how you loved to dance, how I
loved to watch you move with such unselfconscious
grace and, years later, I see you sitting in the hospital

bed in your den when you got too sick
to leave the house. I am holding your hand,
the bones so twisted by rheumatoid arthritis
that you can't hold a pencil. And your feet,

those feet I remember in their black
high-heeled pumps, those feet now so crippled
the bones poke through the skin. Sometimes
I imagine we are all together again, all of us

as we were so often for those noisy Sunday
dinners: my mother serving course after course
of steaming food; all of us with no idea yet
of how much we have to lose.

Nothing Can Bring Back the Dead

I know, but this morning, driving to the university
with my side view mirror improperly adjusted
so I nearly ran into a shiny red Honda
when I was trying to switch lanes, I think

of my mother, dead now twelve years.
I am driving and talking to her, as
though she were in the car with me
as she was when I was a young mother

and I'd pick her up to take her grocery shopping.
And she'd get into my bright blue VW bug,
and she'd be all neat and shiny, clean
as a polished button. She'd hold her handbag,

imitation leather in beige or black with a small
handle and a little clip to hold it closed,
and start right in complaining about my dirty car.
She'd curse in Italian under her breath

as she picked up scraps of paper,
candy wrappers, the assorted refuse of my life
and placed my garbage in a plastic bag
she'd carried to the car for that purpose.

Even as she cleaned up, wrapping the seat belt
around her like a scarf because she couldn't manage
the buckle, she'd tell me how to drive.
"Slow down, watch out for that car, close

the window, there's a draft in this car" –
even when it was a hundred degrees outside.
Then she'd unsnap her purse, that little click
I can still hear in my head, and she'd take out

a hard candy and give it to me. It was always
like that between us. My mother, who could
make me furious, was the one I came to
for comfort, the one who provided whatever

I needed, so today I am driving and talking
to her. I can feel her presence, as though
I were back in her kitchen, sitting
at her round kitchen table, the place

I came to more and more as I grew
older and my children grew. The older she got,
the more people came to her for her wisdom
and earthy humor, her straight talk, her energy,
her ability to laugh, all of us, leaning

on her, my mother who wasn't even
five feet tall, so that at her funeral,
we all sobbed out loud, daughters, sons,
grandchildren, daughters-in-law, sons-in-law,

this Greek chorus of sobbing because how could
someone so strong and alive have vanished?
When I was thirty, I screamed at her
and threw her out of my house for criticizing

my domestic abilities. I fought with her
over everything until, one day, she changed
and I changed, and she became the one
place in the world where I could be safe,
sitting at her table, sipping espresso and talking.
In this car now, I remember the times
she touched my face, "Oh Tesoro," she used to say,
calling me her treasure, and I reach out
for her now, "Tesoro," I say, and
touch her cheek with my hand.

What I Can't Face
About Someone I Love

That my son loves me but would prefer
not to see me too much. Every Sunday night,

when I call him in North Carolina where
he lives with his wife and two children,

I can hear the heaviness in his voice,
his "Hello" tempered with impatience,

our conversation stiff and stilted, though
I always think I can talk to a stone.

Strangers in buses and trains tell me their life
histories, acquaintances tell me about their affairs

and shattered marriages, show me the secret
undersides of their lives. My graduate students vie

for my attention. They want to sit next to me
and carry my bags and fetch my lunch,

but my son can't wait to get off the phone
with me. I ask him how the kids are

or specific questions about school, ask about

his wife, his job. He answers with one or two
words; "They're fine," or "Okay," or "The same."

My son is a lawyer; he was always brilliant
with language, at least written language,

and he can read a three-hundred page book
in an hour and remember every detail,

but with me he turns mute as a stump.
If I ask for help with some legal problem,

he will give it, but I do not hear in his voice
the lilt I hear in my daughter's voice

when I call her. Instead I hear reluctance,
as though his attention were focused

on some truly fascinating person
and he can't wait to get off the phone.

I tell stories that I hope will amuse him,

but finally, after struggling and finding no response,
I can't wait to hang up.

I say, "Well, John, have a good week.
Give everyone a hug for me." I know my son

has divorced me, somewhere deep inside
himself in a place he doesn't look at.

I am too much for him, too loud, too dramatic,
too frantic, too emotional. I laugh too much.

I wear him out in a minute and a half. If he never
saw me again he wouldn't miss me and this is what

I can't face about someone I love.

Is This the Way It Is
Between Mothers and Sons?

Is this the way it is with mothers and sons,
this distance that opens between us like a
canyon I can never bridge? At two, you'd sit
in the wicker laundry basket and watch TV

and play with matchbox cars, your eyes,
gray and clear. We lived in married-student
housing at Rutgers, those Quonset hut houses
with their small square backyards and the

morning glory vine I planted on the chicken
wire fence and the sandbox Grandma bought
for you. I'd watch you play with your Tonka
trucks for hours and hold you in my arms,

your head against my chest, your hair smelling
of Johnson's Baby Shampoo, and I'd read to you,
"One more book, Mom," you'd say. "Just one more."
That's the way it is with mothers and sons,

I swear I could close my eyes and imagine
you are still leaning against me while I read.
As you grew up, each year full of memories,
the boy I drove to track meetings, the way

you ran track every day, though every day
you threw up, other boys so accustomed to it
they didn't seem to notice. Strange how
the days and years spin faster and faster,

the images as you grow away from me
fewer but still clear. Clear until now, years
since you graduated from college and law
school, since your marriage, the birth of your

children, each year the gap between us growing
wider. This is the way it is between mothers
and sons, the mother unable to forget the boy
she held in her arms, the son wanting only

to be the man he's become – lover, husband, father –
and not any woman's son.

Everything We Don't
Want Them to Know

At eleven, my granddaughter looks like my daughter
did, that slender body, that thin face, the grace

with which she moves. When she visits, she sits
with my daughter; they have hot chocolate together

and talk. The way my granddaughter moves her hands,
the concentration with which she does everything,

knocks me back to the time when I sat with my daughter
at this table and we talked and I watched the grace

with which she moved her hands, the delicate way
she lifted the heavy hair back behind her ear.

My daughter is grown now, married
in a fairy-tale wedding, divorced, something inside

her broken, healing slowly. I look at my granddaughter
and I want to save her, as I was not able

to save my daughter. Nothing is that simple,
all our plans, carefully made, thrown into a cracked

pile by the way love betrays us.

At Eleven, My Granddaughter

For Caroline Paige Gillan

At eleven, my granddaughter loves to read,
her long, narrow body stretched out on the sofa,

a book in her hands. She reads for hours.
She takes her hand and gracefully lifts back

her thick, honey-blond hair, tucks it
behind her ear until it falls forward again.

She wears braces and serious glasses with metal frames.
She looks bright and concentrated as a flame.

She sings in a high sweet voice, the way
she sang along with the radio when she was very small,

and she'd ride strapped into her car seat and sing
everywhere they went. Even today, when she gets

into the car, she asks for a specific CD, and she drinks
in the music through all the pores of her skin.

She tells me she wants to be an artist,
and presents me with perfect pictures of animals

she's drawn freehand. Her life, mapped out,
a straight road from Hawkscrest Court in North Carolina

to another house just like her own. When she visits,
she says, "Oh, that's weird," or "You're weird,"

but I shout, "Who wants to be ordinary? How boring!"
and she watches me, as though I were a creature

from Mars, but I hope, years from now,
she'll remember what I've said. I wish her

a long velvet cape lined with scarlet satin,
a life she paints for herself, drawing it freehand,

the strokes of her brush loose and reckless, the picture
emerging, one large bright slash at a time.

My Daughter's Hands

My daughter tells me she has Grandma's hands,
referring to her father's mother who lived with us
for nine years after she had a heart attack. Later,
she went senile and imagined people were coming
out of the TV to get us. She called me over to her

ten times a day to warn me. My daughter's hands
are strong with pronounced veins, and she is convinced
they are her grandmother's. She remembers Grandma
fondly, the way she'd serve bowls of Spaghetti O's,
or count out the meatballs so each child would

have the same number, and how she'd put M&M's
in tin pie plates for them. She does not remember
the grandmother who was so angry finally that she
made a hole in the wall with her rocker,
but rather the woman who cooked bacon for her

and bought Sara Lee cakes. I tell my daughter
I think her hands are like mine, and my hands
come down to me from my mother, the same
square shape, the small fingers. If you looked
at our hands, you'd think we were delicate,

but we never give up, keep working until
we're too sick to move. Sometimes, when I look
at my hand, I imagine my mother reaching
for my hand, as she did so often
when she was still alive, imagine her

hand, brown from all the gardening she did,
tough and calloused, imagine that she is still
sitting with me when I see Dennis, slumped
and broken in his chair, when he says,
"I can't do this anymore," and I use her hands

to give him the courage to go on just as
my daughter uses her hands
to pat my back while I cry.

My Grandson and GI Joe

When he was three, I'd hold my grandson
and kiss his skin, tasting the sweetness that rose
off him. He'd laugh wildly as I made slurping
sounds, while I kissed the soft folds of skin

at his elbow, the bottoms of his wide feet.
My sweet-natured grandson is named Jackson
after a stern Civil War general, and he loves GI
Joe in all his incarnations – GI Joe Warrior and

GI Joe Scuba diver and GI Joe in jungle fatigues
and GI Joe tanks and armored cars, his room
populated with the murderous supplies of war.
My grandson, serious and self-contained, tells

stories to himself while he plays army; he
and his friends shoot tiny rifles, machine guns,
bazookas. They play at war. On TV the real
war is played out, the one where cities

are blasted out of existence, the one where
people die, the one where children are bereft
of arms and legs. My grandson and his friends
wear army fatigue jackets and pants. They chase

each other through the house and fall
elaborately, pretending to be wounded, and then
they rise again to lie flat on the floor and move
the GI Joe figures into action. My grandson

loves beautiful things, satin and velvet,
the smooth stones of my earrings and pendants,
the satin edge of a blanket. He is exuberant,
always thinks he will win the million

dollars promised behind the faces of bottle caps.
He collects tadpoles and holds them with careful
hands. That sweetness still rises off his skin
and emerges from the center of the boy

he has become. GI Joe is a story, a tale
he can create out of imagination and hope.
He doesn't know the exploding missiles on TV
kill people who can't get up, ever, to play again,

or wound soldiers, like those young men in
West Virginia in that article in *The New York Times,*
who went off to Iraq at nineteen, and six
months later returned to their blue-collar town

minus legs and arms, their bodies scarred, their
lives plagued by violent nightmares, so now
they say, "I'm afraid to sleep," and they spend
their nights in the flickering gray light instead,

afraid to close their eyes for fear
of who they'll see.

What We Pass On

For Jackson Stuart Gillan

My son is handsome, like my husband and grandson.
They look like cookie-cutter men, the three of them,

my husband obviously the oldest since his illness
left his face lined and drawn, and my son looks

exactly as his father looked at thirty-seven.
My grandson is a miniature version

of the two of them, but my son and grandson
walk the way I do on my flat feet, chunky

and turned out slightly, only they hit the ground
harder. My grandson emulates his father's walk,

his hands hooked in the pockets of his pants,
his shoulders swinging. Like his father, my son

never gives up. Like me, he needs to heal the world,
needs to be responsible for everyone.

Though my grandson is only seven, he reminds me
of my mother with her exuberant laugh,

her abundant energy, her loving heart, the parts
of all of us, even the ancestors I never met,

caught in my son and grandson. My grandson
trudges into the world on his wide feet, in him

I see my twin. I love the way he loves the feel
of my satin nightgown on his face, the way

he attacks his food with gusto, the way it makes him happy,
the way he looks in his little electric car that he piles

with leftover lumber from the construction site,
and he drives down the hill behind the house,

wearing his hard hat, dumps one load of wood,
goes back for another because he wants to build

a tree house. He drives up the street, stops
at Carina's house, picks her up and they ride off,

as though he had picked her up for a date.
How mixed up this genetic code that sends

my mother back to me in this boy
growing up in North Carolina

so far from any place
my mother had ever seen.

The Dead Are Not Silent

Long after their eyes turn opaque as frosted glass,
their faces still and empty,
long after the gravestones' chiseled faces,
long after the mourners' tears,
the dead return. First, they creep in,
and I imagine I hear a whisper, but when
I turn, there is no one there.

Sometimes it is a touch, light and soft
on my neck, or the lick of cold fingers
on my arm. Gradually, they grow bolder.
They come to my room at night.
I wake up to find them standing above me:

my mother, her face unlined, now a face
from which suffering has been erased.
Her eyes are as full of love as they were
when I could go to her every day.

Sometimes my father is there; his body
seems irrelevant and indistinct, not broken
as it was when he still lived.
I'd visit him every night after Mama died
so he wouldn't be lonely. We didn't

talk much. We'd watch his favorite
program, *Murder She Wrote*. I knew
he was happy to have me there,
as I am happy to have him visit me now.

Finally, my sister appears. She hasn't
even been gone a year. I can tell
she knows I miss her. The room

is crowded with the dead. They move in
and are a comforting presence.
Each day I mention them, remind myself

of something they did or said. I hear them
rustle as they move; their voices, silk scarves
that trail behind me.

What the Dead No Longer Need

The dead no longer need the world
with all its noise and clatter, the people
they loved on earth, their children
and grandchildren, old lovers,
whom they thought they couldn't
live without, the houses they polished
and paid for, the money they gave up
their lives to earn, the cars that made them
feel powerful, all the edges of people
and things no longer sharp and, gradually,
not there at all.

The dead no longer need us, or the world,
all irrelevant in the washed light of that other
place where they live now and where
we can't touch them.

We who are left behind still need them,
want to believe they still love us as they did:
my mother still my mother, my father
still my father, my sister still my sister.
If I reach out I can touch them. I say
their names a dozen times a day.
They do not hear. I imagine
they come back to comfort me, their ghosts
as real as pears in a bowl. But these
are the lies I tell myself.

The dead don't need us anymore.
In that other world they cannot hear us
call them. They have climbed
into a tower where they won't
let down their hair so we can climb it,
so filled we are with our need.

I Want to Celebrate

the small pleasures, the sweet taste of cappuccino
in my mouth, the slow melting of a chocolate square
on my tongue or sitting on a hotel bed
with my twelve-year-old granddaughter,
while we discuss the theme of the movie
we're watching, my granddaughter
with her serious face and her love of books,
the way she carries her book with her
wherever she goes, as I do, and the hug
she gives me when they leave that tells me
she does not want to let me go,
or that moment on the hotel balcony,
my nine-year-old grandson standing near
the railing, leaning his folded arms on it,
and looking out at the skyline of Washington
glowing against the darkening sky,
that moment when I realize
how alike we are, this grandson
whose breath catches when he looks at
the vista stretched out before us. "It makes
you feel so free," he says, both of us
smiling the same way.

The small pleasures, the aroma of basil and mint
at my mother's kitchen door, the heavy feel
of the purple figs from my father's fig tree
in my hand, the loamy smell of my mother's
garden, the glass figurines my daughter
bought me when she was a child,
the bouquet of tulips you gave me
because you knew I loved them, those moments
years ago when we'd walk through the woods together,
hands touching, the times you turn to me
and say, "I don't know what I'd do without you."

Couch Buddha

My daughter calls me Couch Buddha
because people always come to me
for advice and help and
because I give it even when
they don't ask, like my mother did,
because I pushed Paul into finishing
his book proposal,
because I pushed my hairdresser
into demanding respect from her husband,
because people call me on the phone
to ask me what to do,
and I sit on my sofa and tell them –
Couch Buddha who knows
exactly what everyone should do,
poor weak Buddha who eats
the troubles of the world
and answers riddles for everyone
but can't find the way out
for herself.

NEW POEMS

2008

In My Remembered Childhood

In my remembered childhood
it is always summer.
When I think of myself then,
the sun is shining. I walk the rows
of Zio Guilliermo's garden, the tangy
aroma of tomatoes, the loamy smell
of the turned earth, deep and black,
the silk tassels of corn that whisper
in the wind. Sometimes I'd sit
on that dark earth, loving the feel of it
on my fingers and the backs of my legs,
loving the cool place the corn rows made,
telling stories to myself in that safe
and hidden place. During the day,
all the neighborhood children
would gather in the street to play
tag and stickball, Mrs. Cuccinello's
golden retriever barking wildly
behind us, and at night we'd sit
on my back stoop. My mother
wouldn't let us go anywhere else
once dark fell, and in hushed voices
we whispered to one another, the way
friends do, and we'd watch
that Paterson sky. We could see
the chunky stars above our heads
and the fireflies that lit up the night air.
In my remembered childhood,
I am happy, certain that the life
ahead of me will be as safe
and perfumed as the world
I now inhabit and time is a stream
that will never run dry. I have only

to reach out my hand to possess
everything that sparkles and shines
and lights up the dark.

Shame Is the Dress I Wear

On the first day of school, my mother slips a dark blue dress over my head, ties the starched sash. Zia Louisa and Zio Guillermo have come down the back steps to our apartment to see me setting off. They don't have children of their own

and Zio Guillermo is my godfather, so they are a big part of our lives. My mother has starched this cotton dress handed down from Zia Christiana's late in life daughter, Zia Christiana who has enough money to buy lots of pretty

dresses for her red-headed daughter and also throw chickens into the garbage, that year when my father was sick and couldn't work so we lived on farina and spaghetti. When my mother was dying, she talked about seeing those discarded

chickens and about being too ashamed to ask for them. Anyway, I'm standing on that wooden kitchen chair, my mother tugging at the dress, my hair formed into sausage curls that my mother curled by wrapping my thick dark hair

in white rags, my eyes enormous in my long, thin face. Zia Louisa stands back, shakes her head and says, Why didn't you get her a better color? This dress that both my mother and I were proud of until my aunt's comment pointed out what

should have been obvious, that this dark blue color, perfect for a red-head made my white skin look jaundiced. I could almost feel the starched skirt deflate. Sometimes I think that little girl in her navy dress has followed me my whole life through. There she is when I am at a party and I find a chair to sit in and never move or when I am afraid to look in a mirror to see what the years have done to me or when I go to Trinity College to read and I meet the President and his wife,

so slim and Episcopalian, so upper class, the whole place is jammed with faculty dressed in tweed skirts and broadcloth white shirts and leather pumps and shame is the dress I wear that day, shame and that little

girl, that shadow, is there, her head hanging down as it did then, her hands shaking.

City of Memory, Paterson

The city of memory, Paterson, its sky, lavender and purple at dusk, the hills above it, Garret Mountain with its dark face and Lambert castle looking down over the city, its parking lot, the lookout we used to park in when I was in school, the stars over the city, the lights of its buildings, the shadow of NY city in the background while the windows steamed up with our

quick breathing. The city today when I drive down River Street past Our Lady of Lourdes and the Red, White and Blue thrift shop, walk to my building from the lot, past the bail bondsmen signs, and travel agents with signs in Spanish and a flower shop, sporting Spanish words in the windows, past the men in the halfway house next to our building, toothless

men who have the look of old drunks, the seedy-looking young men, their eyes shifting, their hands hanging empty at their sides, this house sad and decrepit where jazz music streams out of the open window each morning. At noon I walk back out of my building, down Ellison to Main where the stores of my youth are gone, replaced by signs that shout

"Dollar Store" and "Bargain" or "Final Going Out of Business Sale," and where in front of each store sits one man on a high ladder to watch the people going in and out of the store to make sure they aren't stealing anything and the clerks who are rude to their customers because they are poor, and I remember Paterson when I was young, Meyer Brothers

Department store with its lovely displays, Chanel #5 perfumes, Naturalizer shoes, creamy leather handbags, its elevator operators who wore white gloves and announced the merchandise on each floor and Quackenbush's Department store, not as fancy as Meyer Brothers but almost, where sometimes we'd stop in the restaurant at the bottom of the curved stair and have an ice cream sundae, though that was later when I was already grown up, and not when I was still a child and my mother would take the three of us, my brother, sister and I downtown while she bought freshly ground coffee in the coffee store and went to pay on time for a refrigerator at

Quackenbush's. When I'd speak to my mother in Italian, she'd say sh-sh and people would pass and say why don't they speak English? They should go back to where they came from, as they do now when people speaking Spanish or Arabic pass by. Once when I was a teenager I went to Quackenbush's with my mother when she was trying to buy

support hose and the clerk was rude and insulting to her, and I stepped in, my voice raised, my arms on my hips, said, "Don't ever speak to my mother or any other customer like that again. I want to speak to the manager." My mother pulled on my arm saying sh-sh, but I wouldn't stop, fury like molten lava taking over my body, my mind, at all the injustice

in the world, at the way being poor and foreign is a crime and the way the poor take it, think they don't deserve anything better, saying sh-sh to their children whose rage finally refuses to be silenced.

It's Complicated, This Loving Now

when it used to be so simple – the way I fell
for you the moment I saw you, that love
at first sight I didn't believe in until I met you,

the sound, smooth as honey, of your voice,
the blue/gray of your eyes, your long fingers plucking
the strings of your guitar, the nimbus of light

that surrounded you, and then, all those years
in between, a series of moments that become
more precious the more I look back at them:

the two of us on our first trip to Italy, your hand
in mine as we walked the streets of Rome and Venice,
the way other people on that trip teased us, saying

"Oh look at the lovebirds," and the more I saw
those others, the more I understood how for them
this trip was about buying things: handbags, shoes,

jewelry, paintings – while for us it was that moment
seeing Michelangelo's David or the Sistine Chapel
or the light falling over Bernini's horses prancing

through their fountain and that we were seeing it
together, our children at home with your mother,
while we took this first trip without

the children, we already married fifteen years
and lucky to find in one another the person
to share theater and books and art and travel.

Sitting at that Café in the Via Veneto at midnight,
we eat gelato with no idea how young we are,
how fortunate, how much we have yet to lose.

How complicated love is now by your illness,
by the way too often I leave you behind
because you cannot travel and I move

like Road Runner through my life though
I cannot escape the frail sound of your voice on the phone
or the shaking I hear when you tell me that you,

who have a PhD and know a million little facts,
forget how to put on your pants. I love you,
you say; I love you, I say back, but how

complicated this loving, mixed as it is
with guilt and shame and with the fear
that this illness will break us both in two.

What Do My Hands Reach For?

I wish I could transport myself through the Catskills, erasing
   the miles between us, and reach for you, I

would do it right this moment, take your body, suddenly
   delicate, in my arms, rest your head

on my chest, stroke your hair. All day the thought of you has
   stayed with me as though your mind were

hands reaching for me, as though you have woken up again
   and it is four a.m. and you call

for me as you did the other night, call
   until your voice is almost gone

and I am not there. I was afraid,
   you said, and I called and called

your name, though I knew you wouldn't hear.
   I thought there was a bearded man in the room

with me. I thought he was going to kill me.
   I knew I was hallucinating again

but it seemed so real.

The Polar Bears Are Drowning

The glaciers are melting.
Polar bears drown; the ice breaks
apart in chunks, and they slide under water.
The surprised bears go under.

We drive through New York state and New Jersey on roads
crowded with SUV's and Hummers and "light" trucks,
spewing pollution into the air. Don't we all think the
other person should conserve our resources? In Italy,
I watch the Italians unplug their appliances, turn off

the hot water heater when they are not using it, walk rather
than drive, and I know that even I, when I go
back to America, I will not do what these people are doing
to try to save the earth. Too much that is green

is covered over with condos and cement, too much of
the world lost to all the objects we desire and believe
we can't live without, No room for bears in New
Jersey, where they have a bear hunt each year

to get rid of the bears though we're the ones who built houses
and took their forests. No room for the deer
which lie dead and mangled on the crowded roads,
all these cars and where are we going?
I watch the bear slide under water. Sorrow. Sorrow.
The world I grew up in is gone and what we pass on to our
children and grandchildren will be so much less than what
we were given, and only our greed and desire to blame.

My Grandchildren in Dallas

My fifteen year old granddaughter says "Natalia is not my friend. I have a lot of acquaintances, but no friends. Natalia is jealous of me, gets angry when I wear new clothes and tells me I look ugly in them." "That's not a friend," I say. "No," she agrees, seriously, "it's not." While her parents are gone on

their trip, I am here in Dallas to take care of Caroline and her eleven year old brother, Jackson. I sometimes think they could take care of me. Jackson tells me how to operate the electrical equipment in the car, helps me put the BMW's shift into gear. He is kind and gentle with me, as though he were my mother

instead of my grandson. After I take Jackson to school in the morning, I straighten the kitchen, prepare what I need to make dinner, take Coco, their tiny dog out, check my mail, and then after lunch, Coco and I take a nap. He curls up next to me on the couch as though he were a cat. After dinner, I

collapse onto the couch as though I had cooked for forty people instead of three, unaccustomed to their huge kitchen, the enormous number of cabinets so that I can't remember where anything is. The appliances are so fancy I can't operate them without written out directions. Still I am happy to be here, to

get to know these grandchildren who have always lived so far away from me, I don't know them as well as I'd like, though I love hugging them, love hearing about their lives, watching them do their homework, knowing that the qualities I remember them having as young children, they still have. My granddaughter's love of books, her sharp intelligence, her quick wit, my grandson's sweet nature, his optimistic outlook, his willingness to help, all these things, only more solidly rooted now in the people they have become, and I'm happy to have these few days with them, hoping in years to come my

grandchildren will remember me with love and fondness as my children remember their grandmothers by telling stories about them that make them both laugh and cry.

Playing with Dolls

When Jennifer and John were little, John played
with GI Joe dolls, Jennifer with Barbie. They'd play
together for hours weaving scenarios where GI Joe
could meet Barbie and they'd ride in her pink car.

Now John's son plays quietly with his GI Joe dolls
and I hear him talking to them, making up scenarios
for those figures the way the children did
when they were little and because I don't see
my grandchildren that much, I see them with an outsider's
eyes and I am afraid for them – Jackson in one room
playing alone, Caroline in the room with us instant
messaging on her laptop and I wonder, looking back,
did our children live so much in their own worlds,
so much space, so lonely?

As a child I played with my brother, using empty plastic
M&M boxes and spools of thread as cars and people
and making up our own worlds, but mostly, we all played
together in the kitchen while my mother cooked and my
father told stories and the house was small and we were
together and in all those years between then and now, how
did we get so much and lose everything?

The Moments That Shine

To Maria and Mario Volpe

On this clear July morning, the skin of the world
is scrubbed and shining. The lemons are big yellow jewels
in the trees; the grapes on the grape arbor hang in clusters
so perfectly formed they could be a work of art, and I am
sitting on my cousin Maria's terrace. Flowers grow all
around us in plaster pots that line the walls. I feel all the
taut strings of my life loosen, the air smooth as scented
cream on my face, and for one moment in these southern
Italian mountains, I could almost be one of the enormous
butterflies that light on the flowers and fly off, so weightless
am I and happy, staring off at the mountains opposite where
San Mauro, my mother's home town, is strung like a
necklace across the mountain tops. Maria brings me an
espresso and pastry she made just for me because I
mentioned my mother used to make it and so she got up at
5 A.M. to start the elaborate process and finished at 12:30,
presenting me with a huge tray of pastechelle drizzled with
honey and sprinkles and I feel welcomed in the place as
though my mother and father were here with me,
leading me home.

How Many Ghosts Can Gather in One House?

Late afternoon, five p.m., that half-light when night
is about to fall but hasn't yet. That's when loneliness
creeps in. Even in a houseful of people, loneliness
is like a scarf that wraps itself around my neck
until I cannot breathe.

My house now is full of nurse's aides and wheelchairs,
walkers and medicine bottles and handymen tramping
up the cellar stairs and through the kitchen in their heavy
boots that leave tracks of dirt and plaster across the floor

But even with all these people, the clatter of pots,
the splash of water in the sink, the clinking of plates
and cups, at five p.m. I am always beset by loneliness,
those moments when I count off all that I've lost – my

mother, father, sister, all claimed by the big hand of death
and without them, these people whose love and care
always kept me safe, how can I keep these dark
shadows from creeping out of the corners of the room,
how can I keep from shivering?

What the Body Knows

I tell my students they have to be vulnerable
as peeled grapes if they want to write,
and this morning, sitting in the IHOP,
I am quivering and exposed
as a peeled grape myself,
my eyes filling with tears,
my daughter's voice on the phone
flat and toneless as a straight line,
though I feel how much effort it takes
for her to say anything at all.
When she hangs up, I know
it is because she is crying
and can't speak. Earlier, I held

my friend's daughter, her blonde hair
pressed to my chest, my hand on her sweet
head, her eyes huge and lovely as pansies
after rain, and I remember holding
my daughter at three in the same way,
this sweetness that rose off her,
and I think how my body keeps inside
itself the sensory memory of holding a child,

how clear that child is to me, though
she is grown now and alone
in her Cambridge apartment,
and how when I held her
and she fell asleep in my arms,
I was so young, I thought this damp
and delicate weight
was all I'd ever have to bear.

Imagine 1979

There we are caught
in a color photograph. Jennifer at seven,
thin and rangy, her hair, recently chopped
off by my sister, has lost all its curls
and now hangs straight around her face.
After that haircut, her hair went from
platinum blonde to a darker color,
like honey. Jennifer never forgave my sister, still mourns
those ringlets springing off her head.

I am thirty-four, wearing the fake leather jacket
my neighbor sewed for me. It is a deep chocolate
brown. I am thin and curvy at the same time;
my hair the color of burnished mahogany, is piled
on top of my head. I look like my daughter does today,
but I don't know it then. When I look at myself
in the mirror, I see only dark skin, dark hair, nothing
beautiful, only a face like a wound. If I could,

I would go back and tell that young woman
how I came to plant my feet
solidly on the ground, to claim my place
as I never could have then, who saw myself
as fragile and easily broken, an outline
yet to be filled in. I try to tell my daughter
now grown and older than I was then,
to find what you love,
what defines you, what turns an insubstantial girl
into a woman certain she knows where
she's going and where she's been.

Acknowledgments

These poems have been previously published in the following journals and anthologies: "People Who Live Only in Photographs," "Little House on the Prairie," "Christmas Story," "I Am Thinking of the Dress," "Do You Know What It Is I Feel," published in *Louisiana Literature;* "There Was No Pleasing My Mother," "Breakfast at the IHOP," "Your Voice on the Phone Wobbles," "I Walk Through the Rooms of Memory," published in *Connecticut Review;* "Superman," "Selective Memory," published in *Prairie Schooner;* "Nighties," published in *New Letters;* "Trying to Get You to Love Me," "In the Movies No One Ever Ages," "On Thanksgiving This Year," published in *LIPS;* "My Father's Fig Tree Grew in Hawthorne," "Nothing Can Bring Back the Dead," "Couch Buddha," published in *VIA: Voices In Italian Americana;* "Spike-Heels," "At Eleven," "My Granddaughter," published in *Feminist Studies;* "What Did I Know About Love," published in *Edison Literary Review;* "I Want To Write a Poem to Celebrate," published in *Haight Ashbury Literary Journal;* "My Sister and Frank Sinatra," published in *Sinatra Anthology;* "My Father Always Drove," published in *Asphodel;* "The Photograph of Us on an Outing to Cold Spring," published in *Paddlefish;* "Driving Into Our New Lives," "What the Dead No Longer Need," published in *Pennsylvania English.* Some of the poems in this volume appeared previously in *Flowers from the Tree of Night* (Chantry Press, Midland Park, NJ, 1980, 1981); *Winter Light* (Chantry Press, 1985, 1987); *The Weather of Old Seasons* (Cross-Cultural Communications, Merrick, NY, 1988, 1993); *The Dream Book: Writings by Italian-American Women (edited by Helen Barolini: Schochen, NY, 1985); From the Margin: Writings in Italian Americana (edited* by Paul Giordano, Anthony Tamburri and Fred Gardaphé, Purdue University Press, 1990); *Il viaggio delle donne* (edited by Giovanna Capone and Denise Nico Leto, Sinister Wisdom, 1990); *The Voices We Carry* (edited by Mary Jo Bona, Guernica Editions, Montreal-Toronto, 1994); *On Prejudice* (edited by Daniella Gioseffi, Doubleday, NY, 1993); *La Bella Figura: Choices* (Malafemmina Press, San Francisco, 1993); *Speaking for Peace* (edited by Ruth Jacobs, 1993); *Cries of the Spirit* (Boston, Beacon Press, 1991); and the following journals: *Poetry Australia, LIPS, North Dakota Quarterly, Negative Capability, Voices in Italian Americana, La Bella Figura, Slow Dancing, The Croton Review, The Journal of Women and Spirituality, Studia Mystica, The Passaic Review, The Chester Jones Foundation Awards Anthology, Almanacco, Trapani Nuovo, La Terza Pagina, The New Moon Review, Free Inquiry, Earth's Daughters, Ora Madre, Sri Chinmoy Awards Anthology.* Some of the poems in this book have been published previously in the following anthologies and magazines: *Gifts of the Fathers* (ed. T. R. Verney, Crossings Press, 1992); *Identity Lessons: An Anthology of Contemporary Writing About Learning to Be American* (Penguin/Putnam, 1999); *The Christian Science Monitor; The New York Times; Poetry Ireland; LIPS Magazine; Many Mountains Moving; Connecticut Review; The New Renaissance; MSS; Negative Capability; The Red Brick Review; Voices in Italian Americana; Vivace,* and *Controlled Burn.* The following poems have been published previously: "Donna Laura," "These Are the Words I Have Said," "When I Was a Young Woman" in *Prairie Schooner,* 2001; "Poem to My Husband of Thirty-three Years" in *Connecticut Review,* Spring 1999. "Something I Always Wanted But Didn't Get" in *Connecticut Review,* Fall 1999. "Since Laura Died" and "A Geography of Scars" in *Connecticut Review,* Fall 2001. "What I Didn't Learn in School" in *Rattle,* 2001. "The Cup," "Song in Praise of Spring," "Return," "The Softness of Snow," "Rainbow Over the Blue Ridge Mountains," "Is This What It's Like?" in *Christian Science Monitor,* 1999, 2000, 2001. "Fourteenth Christmas" in *LIPS* magazine, Issue 21. "The Bed," "In the Stacks of the Paterson Public Library," and "Phone Calls" in *LIPS,* Issue 23, September, 2000. "Nonno," in *Corragio* (Women's Press). "Laura, Now That You Are Gone" and "Talking About Underwear," in *Long Shot,* Vol. 24, 2001. "Water Chestnut" and "When I Leave

You" in *VIA (Voices in Italian Americana)*, Spring 2001 (Vol. 12.10) and Fall 2001(Vol. 12.2). "The Dodge Silver Hawk" in *SOLO*, 2002. "In the Pages of a Photo Album" in *the new renaissance*, Fall 2000, issue 33. "The Secret I Would Tell," "Shame," and "How to Turn a Phone Call into a Disaster" in *Prairie Schooner*, 2002. "My Father Always Bought Used Cars" in *The Southeast Review*, Vol. 21, Number 2, Spring 2002. "Learning to Love Myself," "The Dead Stay with Us" and "The Herald News" in *VIA*, 2002. "Poem to Jennifer" and "My Mother Who Could Ward Off Evil" in *Connecticut Review*, Spring 2003. "This Time Last Year, Trying Not to Think," "Out the Window, If I Were a Magic Fixer," and "Growing Pains" in *LIPS*, Issue 25, 15, Number 3, Spring 2002. "My Grandchildren in Dallas," in *LIPS*, Issue 28/29, 2007-2008. "It's Complicated, This Loving Now," *Louisiana Literature*, Fall-Winter, 2002. "Shame Is the Dress I Wear," in *Rattle*, Volume 14, No. 1, Summer 2008. "What the Body Knows," in *Prairie Schooner*, Vol. 81, No. 4, Winter 2007.

In *What We Pass On: Collected Poems: 1980-2009,* Maria Mazziotti Gillan weaves a tapestry of one woman's life – wife, mother, grandmother, daughter, grand-daughter, Italian American. Reading these poems in one volume makes us acutely aware of how memory is layered, each new poem adding another detail, another color, another perspective so that we watch as the poet and the people around her change. With increasing clarity and honesty, Gillan peels away all the self-protective layers and invites us in so we can see in her story a reflection of our own. Her work in all its texture and exuberance, its passion and power, forces us to care about what matters and teaches us to be human. This is a poet who, in these courageous poems, shows us why poetry matters and why it can change us.

Maria Mazziotti Gillan is the Founder and the Executive Director of the Poetry Center at Passaic County Community College in Paterson, NJ. She is also the Director of the Creative Writing Program and a Professor of Poetry at Binghamton University-State University of New York. She has published eleven books of poetry, including *The Weather of Old Seasons* (Cross-Cultural Communications), and *Where I Come From, Things My Mother Told Me,* and *Italian Women in Black Dresses* (Guernica Editions). She is co-editor with her daughter Jennifer of four anthologies: *Unsettling America, Identity Lessons,* and *Growing Up Ethnic in America* (Penguin/Putnam) and *Italian-American Writers on New Jersey* (Rutgers). She is the editor of the *Paterson Literary Review.* Her newest book *All That Lies Between Us* (Guernica Editions, 2007) was given the American Book Award.